DARIUS COOPER was born in Pune and got his first Master's in Literature and Aesthetics from Bombay University. He taught at the SIES College in Sion, Bombay, from 1972 to 1979. In 1980, he left for the US on a scholarship to pursue further studies at the University of Southern California in Los Angeles. In 1982, he got a second Master's degree in English from USC and in 1989 he got a PhD in Literature and Film from USC. He currently resides and teaches Critical Thinking, Humanities and Film in the English Department of San Diego Mesa College.

He has authored *Between Tradition and Modernity: The Cinema of Satyajit Ray* and *In Black and White: Guru Dutt and Hollywood Melodrama. Beyond the Chameleon's Skill,* a volume of poems was published in 20

THE FUSS ABOUT QUEENS AND OTHER STORIES

DARIUS COOPER

OM
Om Books International

Published in 2014 by

OM

Om Books International

Corporate & Editorial Office
A-12, Sector 64, Noida 201 301
Uttar Pradesh, India
Phone: +91 120 477 4100
Email: editorial@ombooks.com
Website: www.ombooksinternational.com

Sales Office
4379/4B, Prakash House, Ansari Road
Darya Ganj, New Delhi 110 002, India
Phone: +91 11 2326 3363, 2326 5303
Fax: +91 11 2327 8091
Email: sales@ombooks.com
Website: www.ombooks.com

Cover photograph courtesy *Mumbai: Where Dreams Don't Die* by Raghu Rai

ISBN: 978-93-84225-60-5

10 9 8 7 6 5 4 3 2 1

Printed in India

CONTENTS

INTRODUCTION

Every short story has to inevitably become a clean, well-lighted space. But from where should it emerge? Does it reside somewhere? Does it have to be coaxed? And then, like Plato's (un)fortunate cave-dweller who breaks his chains and emerges for the first time and casts his eyes on the sun, should the story ascend to meet that sun or have doubts and retreat back into the darkness of that cave from which it had crawled out? As a storyteller I don't have all the answers. They are there and in order to find them, you will have to excavate them from where they are buried in each story.

For me, asking apocalyptic questions is more important than providing the quintessential answers. So, who have been my real teachers who have taught me how to write stories effectively? They are, in fact, all the interesting human beings that I have encountered in one way or another, so far, in my life.

From the family fold, let me first extract my late mother and father, both of whom were superb storytellers. My mother was not educated. My father read a lot. In the last very painful nights and days of their lives, the only way I could make them forget their individual fatal ailments was to find a way and almost trick both of them to tell me stories about their past: how they met, fell in love, who their first boyfriends and girlfriends were, what was their Poona and Bombay like—and the miracle I was hoping for always happened.

The groaning, mean, and spiteful patients would suddenly be transformed into wise, philosophical, generous and clever storytellers and one would joyously be taken far away from their room into other spaces where one would cease to smell the harsh air of medicines and mercurochrome. Instead, there would be flowers and fruits and food, accompanied by jokes and laughter and togetherness.

The other storytellers I have learnt from were often accidental people, like Ishaaq, the Bhusawal Railway Colony barber, who visited every officer's bungalow and in his garden, gave him and all his *baba*s a special haircut. Every inch and foot of hair was cut to the accompaniment of a fabulous story. It would inevitably start from the *mohalla* where Ishaaq had his tiny shop. Then it would spread and magically fill up all his pilgrimages to every bungalow from whose individual arteries he would extract, prune, and shape an interesting narrative. This would be verbally enacted inside our heads as his skillful fingers orchestrated the scissors outside our skulls.

And finally there are my friends who I regularly visit, especially the Bombay-based ones, for four weeks every winter and for six weeks every summer. And when we sit down to exchange stories, I trick them into narrating all those old stories of all our intimate adventures that I had shared with them. After those are exhausted, I prompt them to tell me new stories involving all those experiences where I am absent. And even when I have heard these a thousand times, there is always something new that is added and pondered over and shared, lovingly and willingly.

Once started, like Scheherazade, they refuse to stop. But what is so special to all these storytellers and to all their stories is their insistence that every story worth telling has to begin from some extraordinary premise or thesis. The ordinary just has no place in any good story. Yet, this extraordinary moment, or thought, or utterance, or action, has to be, above all, genuine. It cannot be faked, exotic, or deliberately imposed upon the narrative by any creative device of cleverness. It has to emerge from an authentic centre, or what existential philosophy defines as being always "in good faith". And once that is established, it has to be developed along lines where all kinds of powerful epiphanies are discovered and created, and once these happen, then they have to be actively engaged and speculated upon in order to arrive at that clean, well-lighted space.

So, it is in tribute to these great storytellers that I offer you mine, and in case you spot echoes and refrains from accomplished masters like Joyce, Chekhov, Hemingway, Carver (to name just a few), kindly remember they always came, afterwards!

Since a majority of the stories are placed in the Parsi milieu, let me express the Parsi intent behind such a presentation. Let me begin at the very beginning to explore, via these stories, why I do not feel comfortable within my own community as one of its historically placed subjects.

I was born in Dr. Coyajee's Parsi Hospital in Poona on November 9, 1949. I lived with my mother and sister with my mother's youngest brother Rusy in his two tiny *chawl* rooms at 2394 Sholapur Road. So I began my Parsi existence as a *chawl Parsi*. It is here that I spent the happiest days of my childhood till my uncle married a rich man's Parsi daughter who came and expelled us into a series of unhappy periods (more of this later).

It was as a *chawl* Parsi, living with other poor Parsis and generous Irani and Sindhi families that I witnessed the finer side of these poor people in general and the Parsis in particular. Our Irani landlady, who owned the entire *chawl* and Prince Restaurant had literally brought up my mother and her younger brother when they had been suddenly orphaned at 12 and 16 years of age. So rents lapsing for months, and food being always put on our table, and clothes (especially the terelyne ones stitched by Sindhis in Hong Kong) for me and my sister to last through the months always appeared as miracles, especially on auspicious Parsi New Year days like Navroze and Pateti. We never had to wait for Christmas when Santa Claus came laden with presents for the world. We had our own Iranian and Sindhi *farishtas*.

Our immediate neighbour was old Mehramai who existed solely on the funds provided by several Bombay Parsi charitable organisations for taking care of her older brother Dinsajee, a brilliant lawyer who tragically went insane when his beloved did not turn up on the wedding day and was never heard from again. What was remarkable about Mehramai was that the doors and windows of her *chawl* residence were never shut. The reason was that her two tiny rooms were always occupied by scores of poor Hindu families that lived far away in Poona's rustic suburbs like Hadapsur, Urli, Loni. These poor families came to the city of Poona every week to sell whatever they grew on their farms and while the men plied their trade in the Camp Market, their wives worked as domestic servants in the buildings of the wealthy on Main Street and East Street and elsewhere. They left all their belongings with Mehramai who they adopted as their Mother India. They slept on her floor. They bathed and washed their clothes in her bathroom and they arranged and prayed before their countless gods distributed generously in all those Mehramai corners that would accept them. She did not charge them a single old or *naya paisa*. She even babysat their abundant children who in fact were my early companions with whom I played *gilli-danda* and *kabaddi* and marbles, and who taught me how to make *manjha* during the kite season.

Our first expulsion from this 2394 Sholapur Road Eden sent us to 3 Sholapur Road where my paternal grandfather and his second wife resided. Both turned out to be monsters and witches of the highest magnitude, and in the repeated cruelties they practised on my parents, my sister, and myself, they showed me for the first time the sinister side of human nature. For the first time, I saw many contradictions, and being continuously victimised, made a resolve that one day I would let the rest of the world know how my family and I had suffered. My stories are hence, proof of such occurrences.

But there are other Parsi encounters that still have to be placed before the readers. I migrated to Bombay in 1966 and for three years lived as a paying guest in another *chawl* in Grant Road belonging to one of the brothers of my grandfather who had been kicked out by his wife and sons after they had all migrated to England. In exchange for the airfare provided by my kind father for his impending return to Bombay, he promised to look after me for a small monthly sum of money as I commenced my academic career at St. Xavier's College.

This man, however, turned out to be even a bigger monster who took out all his suppressed revenge and rage on his sons and family by finding me as the unfortunate substitute. But while enduring my precarious Dickensian existence with him, I often sought relief by comparing my pain with the overwhelming poverty, cruelty, hardness, and the sheer victimisation of the other Parsis who lived in that same Dubash building, and the insidious and strange violence they daily imposed upon each other.

In St. Xavier's, however, I confronted two very different kinds of Parsis. First, there were the *baugh* Parsis where most of the men displayed obnoxious behavioural tendencies and were obsessed with the idea of a sham masculinity that was built on a repertoire of hundreds of memorised jokes that would be offered spontaneously to fit and comment all occasions. Not only was this exercise very tedious, redundant and boring, but many times the jokes became racist and offensive, especially, when a lot of other Indian communities were disgustingly parodied in them in the form of vulgar revisions that were then recited and sung to the tunes of popular Hindi film songs. The *baugh* women did not participate in this and were demure and mostly well behaved. Nor did they offer any criticism to this consistently enacted odious ritual which they seemed to secretly enjoy.

Then there were, what I would call, the very privileged Parsis. These lived in Bombay's famous Art Deco buildings with Romantic English and European names like Ivorine, Belvedere Court, Sans Souci. These were the Art Deco Parsis whose well-mannered and sophisticated daughters were regularly driven to college and back in their polished chauffeured cars. However, when their daughters sat for their final exams, the parents nervously waited in their parked cars with numerous snacks and tons of eau-de-cologne bottles especially for those nervous ones who regularly vomited before entering the exam hall and repeated it hours later when exiting it.

The villa Parsis were their cousins who lived in large mansions on Warden and Napeansea Roads, and always seemed to *descend* from their homes onto our level. Many of them were very snobbish, and not particularly bright. But what they prided themselves most on was painstakingly mimicking that life left behind by the British. They read only British literature and had an enormous knowledge of European western classical music. They belonged to exclusive British-founded clubs like The Elphinsone, the Willingdon and the Cricket Club of India. Their homes were run like museums, full of exquisite paintings and statues. One had to walk carefully in almost each room, since most of the artifacts were considered very rare expensive family heirlooms and if they trembled even very slightly while we walked, we were told, softly, of course, to leave the room.

It was then that I wondered whether the Parsi community had any intrinsic worth of its own. The Bengalis, the

Maharashtrians, the Tamilians, the Muslims, the Christians (to name a few) all *had* their own intrinsic essences and values. They had their own language, their own music, their own literature, and their own idiosyncratic culture and mannerisms in practically everything they thought, felt, and did. The Parsis by comparison had none. Their language was borrowed from Gujarat and their lifestyle was a carefully rehearsed mimicry of the British. Except for their food, there was nothing that could inclusively be called Parsi. And even the culture they had managed to salvage from their traditional home of Parse in Iran still remains largely enigmatic and unexplained. Take our Parsi prayers and sacred *gathas*, which are memorised and practised as rituals on a daily basis. But what they mean, who wrote them, and why they have to be recited in particular ways—no Parsi is genuinely interested in probing these issues. As long as they are performed, that is all that matters.

That is why I feel like a complete outsider. There is no way I can either define or reside in my so-called Parsi skin. And the only way I can try to overcome this daily homelessness is to shed it repeatedly, thereby creating a critical distance, and then using my role as a writer, to try and understand this fascinating and strange enigma which the world in general and India in particular categorises as *the* Parsi.

Finally, I would like to acknowledge the journals in which some of these stories first appeared:

'His Omelette and Her *Tandava*' appeared in *Weber Studies: A Special Issue on South American Litt/Culture. Vol. 15. No 1. Winter, 1988*, from Weber State University;

'The Fuss About Queens' was awarded First Place Winner, 1997, when it was entered for 'Katha: The Indian American Fiction Conest' sponsored by *India Currents* and *The Asian Pacific, America Journal.* It was published in the latter's *Journal, Vol. 6. No. 2. Fall/Winter, 1997*;

'Says Trivikarma, "It's all a Question of Height"' appeared in *The International Quarterly, Vol. 1. No. 2., 1993*, from Atlanta, Tallahassee, Washington;

'144 Tughlaq Kutir' appeared in *The Bombay Literary Review, 1990. Vol. 2.*, from Bombay;

'Pestonji's Tower of Silence' appeared in *The Massachusetts Review: Special Issue on South Asian Expatriate Writing. Vol. XXIX. No. 4., Winter 1988-1989;*

'When Still Life Still Moves' appeared in *Indian Horizons. Vol. XXXII. No. 4., 1983* from New Delhi;

'The Dance Lesson' appeared in *The Daily*, 1983, Bombay.

I am also very grateful to my typist, Mary Ann, who cheerfully retyped this manuscript and to my editor, Dipa Chaudhuri, for scrupulously editing each story and giving me interesting suggestions to improve it.

Darius Cooper
San Diego, California

THE METAPHORICAL SPOT

Neelkantha decided to kill himself the day his wife suddenly announced at the dining table that she was going to take fencing lessons. "Way to go, Ma, way to go," his teenage son and daughter responded in unison. He tried to join in, but as usual, his voice fell on deaf ears. Neither Jyoti, his wife, nor Satya, his son, nor Meenakshi, his daughter, bothered to laugh when he suggested cleverly, "Now we shall have our own Nadia in the family."

It wasn't that they were unfamiliar with this yesteryear's popular stunt queen of all those crazy Homi Wadia swashbuckling films that the recent video explosion had popularised once again in the living rooms of Bombay. "It's so passé, Dad," was all that Meenakshi said. "Your dad's *certainly* most passé," Jyoti confirmed. Then with a combined "Excuse me", all three got up from the table and left the room, ruefully shaking their heads.

Left all alone once again, Neelkantha looked at the remnants of the last supper around him. Slowly getting up from his chair, he went to his room. He knew what he had to do. His liberation lay in that blue ink bottle, sitting invitingly on his study table. Picasso's Blue Period would be nothing compared to the one he was about to impose on himself.

It was really Satya who had provided him with what he secretly referred to as that fatal Socratic instinct. These days Socrates and Nadia swam in the same Neelkantha bloodstream.

Satya had been working on a school chemistry project related to "Poisons and Dangerous Toxins". Back home early from work one day, Neelkantha had eavesdropped on one of Satya's phone conversations. He was waxing eloquent to one of his buddies about a poison he had recently experimented with, following instructions from a foreign journal. "It doesn't kill you instantly, *yaar*. It takes 12 hours. Long enough for it to make an entire tour of your body. Yeah, yeah, but I want to see its effects on an animal first. A human specimen would have been perfect, *yaar*. Listen, do you have one in your house? You don't? Come on, *yaar*. Every Indian house has at least one candidate. What? In my house? *Arrey*, Dad would instantly qualify. And he would pass the test with flying colors as well. *Achha*, listen, I'll wait for you at the corner. Pick me up in 15 minutes. Bye."

After Satya had left on his skateboard, Neelkantha had quickly slid into his son's room with an empty ink bottle. He recollected how his children laughed at his old-fashioned preference for ink over the ball-point. When he did graduate to the ball-point, they laughed some more, this time, at his inability to work on the word-processor.

Now laughing to himself, he found 24 samples of the poison Satya had talked about neatly stacked on his table. Carefully taking a few drops from each so that Satya would not get suspicious, Neelkantha filled his bottle and silently retreated into his room. This was the only place where he felt comfortable.

In the past he had often sneaked into his children's rooms many times to capture or recover (he didn't know which) a sense of fatherly belongingness from the objects which they handled every day. Several times he had cradled Satya's skateboard or passed his fingers lovingly over Meenakshi's Jane Fonda physical fitness videos. He wondered when was the last time he had actually seen Satya walking. And Meenakshi's obsession with her body was literally turning her into a statue.

He speculated whether kids nowadays were actually born with any umbilical cords. And if they were, they seemed to cut them off drastically in the womb itself. Of course, they found new umbilical wires, like his kids had. They were always wired to some gadget or the other.

Neelkantha laughed. He remembered his father, who went everywhere with his prayer beads in one hand and the Gita in the other. Now, his kids were either glued to their iPods or their cell phones. And at home, they were either absorbed in domesticating their selectively collected TV and video images or surrendering onanistically to their video games that just made them come as they went on and on and on...

Technology seemed to have taken them over so completely that many times Neelkantha felt he could not possibly be either their skeletal or their flesh-and-blood father. They obeyed only the TV. It told them how to dress, brush their teeth, drink the right drink, eat the right food, what film to see, what musical concert to attend; in short: how to be a *dude* or how to be a *chick* in their peers' eyes.

Humorously, he started making a postmodern inventory: iPods, phones, cable, TV and videogames had already programmed their minds and cultivated their attitudes. Then came all the shampoos, lotions, soaps, creams and perfumes that soon took over all their senses. There was no question here of the outer mind and the inner mind reacting to any external or internal stimuli. Thinking was merely an extinct animal that threatened never to awaken from its hibernation. What mattered most was how much of their bodies should be revealed and how much should be concealed and it was all decided, finally, either by some famous music channel or by some hotshot *kapda guru*.

"Please don't show your ignorance," Jyoti had reprimanded him once. "Kids are more sophisticated and open about sex now. It's not sex they have to worry about. It's AIDS. You know what that is, don't you? They have to keep away from the HIV Positives, even when their hormonal vibes synchronise in a crowded dance-filled room."

It was amazing how effortlessly Jyoti had moved into the 21st century. She was already talking its language, thinking its thoughts, and feeling its feelings. Maybe Indian women could vibe with their present better than dinosaurs like him because of the terrible victimisation they had suffered at their men's hands. By joining their more democratic children, they seemed to avenge themselves on men like him. But why on earth would she want to take fencing lessons? To rival her daughter's aerobic routines or to strike a pose like Madonnabai had?

Answers were never easy and it was futile to ask so many questions since no one bothered to answer them anyway.

Neelkantha quickly unscrewed the ink bottle and drank the poison. It was 20 minutes past. Now that death had finally entered him, the next question was, where should it end its journey? The absurdity of that thought made him suddenly gag with laughter. He decided to stretch out on his bed. But then he got up. He did not want to die stretched out like a corpse on his bed! He did not want to die in this house! *That* death had already occurred at the hands of his family. If his life had had no significance, his death had to find one. He had to die in such a way so that his family would be forced *not* to forget it. Ever!

"That's it. That's it," he whispered to himself. "I have 12 hours to roam this *ajnabi* city of mine. Twelve hours is, I think, sufficient time for me to find that exact metaphorical spot. And once I find it, I shall arrange my death on it. I'll show them. I'll show the whole damned lot of them."

But to find that metaphorical spot in Bombay, he knew, would not be easy.

This city that he belonged to had changed so much. Every day he found himself not recognising what used to once be so familiar, so heartwarming, about Bombay. Where was all this change coming from? He felt himself at first being slowly cheated, and then literally becoming extinct.

Twelve hours was all he had. Yes. Twelve hours to find that all-important fold within which he could leave some traces of his final definitive extinction.

Neelkantha stepped out of his housing society. He was thankful to see Haribhau's son, Peeraji, still repairing shoes over his late father's anvil. His kids never bothered to send their shoes for repair. Only he did. They simply threw them away. They were horrified when, one day, he had suggested that instead of throwing their old shoes out, they could give them to the servants. "That would be such an insult, Dad. Our servants can afford to buy new ones with the money we pay them," Meenakshi had nonchalantly explained.

This exchange had taken place when she was going through one of her phases. She was always going through some phase or the other. Neelkantha laughed. When was the last time that, as a father, he had actually succeeded in having the last word?

He slowly approached Peeraji who was roughly around Satya's age. Unlike Haribhau who had always done a better job with a shoe when he had been under the influence of the local hooch, Peeraji was a sober young man. He was diligent, industrious, and it was rumoured that he had a lot of other small *naukris* behind this ostentatious front of being the housing society's favoured *mochi*.

Neelkantha took off his waist belt and asked Peeraji to punch some additional holes in them. After the young man had punched three, he gave Neelkantha his belt and politely asked for three rupees. Neelkantha was taken aback. "You know, young man, your father had once punched five holes for me in another belt, and when I had started to pay him, he had scolded me. I still remember his words: "*Arrey, sahib*, I had actually made belts for your father from the finest *chamda*. We had even drunk *chai* from the same cup and *pelate*. How can you insult me now by poking holes in our relationship with *paisa*? *Chee, chee*."

"Arrey, sahib," Peeraji retorted, mimicking his late father. "It was because of such generosity that my father went so quickly to the burning *ghat* at Chandanvadi. And where *was* your father when mine was being carried to be burnt? Probably having *angrezi* tea at the Oberoi Sheraton. My father, never separated *naukri* from *dosti*. That was his problem. If he had, he wouldn't have been so full of holes when he died. If there is one thing this city of ours has taught me, *sahib*, it's that every hole here has its price."

A group of neighbouring cab drivers listening to Peeraji broke out in a round of applause. All of them appeared to be these new smart young men who went to night school or attended those several language classes that were mushrooming in Indian neighbourhoods to better themselves in order to improve their livelihoods.

Neelkantha remembered that cab driver who had spoken to him in fluent English one day and had gone on to inform him proudly that he was even fluent in French. "They call me *Phoreen Ek Numbari*, sir. All the big hotels in Bombay call for my services, especially when they have large numbers of tourists. Now I am learning German and Italian as well."

While Neelkantha had found this aspect very enterprising, it had pained him when a little later the same cab driver had revealed that his intelligence did not always go hand in hand with his emotions.

One evening, Neelkantha had been asked by Jyoti to stay away from the home because she was entertaining some very important women friends. When Neelkantha had protested, Jyoti had flicked tea at him and labelled him, all in one breath, as "a reactionary and a chauvinist".

Agitated and upset, Neelkantha had ordered that young cab driver's taxi, and when he had arrived, had asked him to drive him to the all-night West End Bar. "Pick me up at 2 a.m. will you? And if I'm drunk, please bring me back to Flat 303 and knock on the servant's door. They'll do the rest."

That nice young driver had quickly stopped the cab and in a quiet but firm voice had asked Neelkantha to "Get out, please."

Stung by such a reaction, Neelkantha had exploded, "But I'll pay you double, you swine. Just because you know so many languages does not..."

"Please don't be abusive, sir," the young man had calmly retorted. "I don't carry drunks. I have a reputation to maintain. Everyone knows me at the West End. Besides, no one likes to ride in a taxi that smells of fart and vomit. Kindly, get out, sir, and ask some Dharavi-type *taxiwala* to take charge of you."

Later, nursing his drinks, Neelkantha had suddenly remembered his old drinking comrade Trivedi, the small-causes lawyer. Trivedi, however, did have a wonderful Dharavi-type *taxiwala* who would religiously take the drunken lawyer every night to his ramshackle one-room flat at Dockyard Road, unlock his door, spread him out on his bed, literally like a corpse, lock the door after him, put the key under the Ganesh idol at the entrance and dutifully leave. Now, *that* kind of dedication was practically non-existent these days.

Ordering his sixth whiskey, Neelkantha remembered that night when he and that faithful Dharavi-type *taxiwala* had expressed simultaneous astonishment when after opening the back door of the taxi, they had suddenly found good old Trivedi missing. Neelkantha remembered running up and down the pavement. He and the Dharavi-type *taxiwala* had argued that they *had* put Trivedi in the backseat *together* just half an hour ago!

Suddenly cries of "Help!" emanating from a deep manhole beside the pavement had cleared up the mystery. The drunken Trivedi had stepped straight out of the taxi and into the same manhole over which one of his clients was suing the local Mazagon Municipality for the past one month. In fact, Trivedi won the case quite convincingly by merely appearing in court the next day, swathed in bandages, his injuries piling up all the legal points in his client's favour without the assistance of any legal jargon on his part.

The noise of the crowd pouring out of the day's first matinee show from the ugly renovated Metro movie palace brought him back from that manhole moment. Neelkantha remembered his own tears when he saw the contractor's cruel demolition balls thumping the old Metro walls and bringing them down like the walls of Jerico in D.W. Griffith's epic. What intolerance!

That whole week had been a very cruel one for Neelkantha. "Can you imagine a grown man crying over a building," Jyoti had tittered at the dining table. "What was so damned special about that old derelict edifice, anyway?" she had demanded, slipping cruelly into that old form of English that these days had been made extinct by the fast-food syllables and the latest abbreviations of email. "It was not the building, foolish woman," Neelkantha had snapped back, "it was a whole way of life." "Then why the fuss?" Satya had interjected. "When something that was cool no longer is, so be it. One should only live for now, Dad."

Admiring his son's nonchalant utterance, Neelkantha had replied. "You know, there was a time when even cynicism had a lot of passion." His son's casual way of dismissing history had now really stoked his anger. "What about all this?" he had remarked. "Where do all your yesterdays go to? Don't you ever want to, in your techno terminology, rewind? Or do you want to live in a permanent fast-forward? No wonder you don't walk but always use the skateboard. All that you kids are interested in is going from point A to point B. What happens in between is not important." "It's better if life *is* a blur, Dad," Meenakshi had chipped in. "Our generation doesn't believe in nostalgia." "Why should it," he had riposted, "since the present is all taken care of and provided for. O, what's the use of talking."

For a while, Neelkantha sat on the bus-stop bench staring at this horrible matchbox monstrosity they dared to still call a palace. He looked at the garishly painted marquee bulging with the latest trash from Hollywood. The Hollywood lion that had once roared from its grandiose centre had now become a rabid mongrel, frothing at the mouth in Dolby sound. He remembered so well the courteous Parsi and Goan ushers in their impeccable MGM uniforms. He could still visualise the Muslim soda-jerk *chacha* behind the marble soda fountain, never spilling a drop as he made your ice cream soda for you during the 15-minute interval. These were men who loved the cinema and had a prodigious knowledge of Western films. They could hum all those complicated Max Steiner and Bernard Hermann scores; repeat all those great lines, especially from tongue-in-cheek film-noirs; and even argue about the talented Anthony Mann being a much better director of Westerns than the highly overrated John Ford.

He could still see those wonderful Technicolor printed notices and posters that the squint-eyed manager Mr. Tavaria would hand out to him every week announcing all the forthcoming attractions. This was when Neelkantha was staying in his father's house which boasted a splendid balcony.

In order to advertise their upcoming attractions at the Metro Palace, Mr. Tavaria's men would come every week and stretch a new banner across their balcony and the Goan Institute building's opposite. Instead of charging money, Neelkantha's father, on his son's behalf, had made a deal with Mr. Tavaria. He would ask nothing more than all that wonderful promotion material that Hollywood and certain vested interests like Max Factor, sent out to the theatres those great American moguls had built in some of Asia's biggest cities to promote their latest film products internationally.

Neelakantha sighed. One day, in a fit of rage, his foolish wife had sold all the splendid memorabilia to the *raddiwala*. That had hurt him deeply. She was not a sentimental woman, but her instincts made her embrace the present with such violence that sometimes it frightened him. Satya and Meenakshi were never really close to her, but she was determined never to embarrass them. She always tried to gain their approval. She read the magazines they read. She listened to the music they danced to. And she consumed the films and videos they saw. She developed an instinctive cunning to "hike up her percentage" with her kids by constantly victimising him, and that too, in their presence.

Neelkantha smiled to himself. A phrase had suddenly parachuted on him during a dinner Jyoti had once dragged him to. Someone had coined the phrase which became his wife's favourite. He forgot who it was, but he remembered those words well. They seemed to pierce him still like an epitaph. "You, Neelkantha, are the last bastion of modernism being pulverised by the collective postmodern fury of your own family."

The poison in his body was making his throat feel dry. Neelkantha got up. He longed to drink a large glass of fresh sugarcane juice made the old-fashioned way. There was a row of fruit juice stands on the pavement opposite, but he did not feel like going into any one of them. He wanted to drink sugarcane juice that would be squeezed between two vertical iron cylinders that were manually operated. He hated tasting juice that came out of the electric whir of blenders and plastic containers. Besides, today's fruits had acquired postmodern identities too! They seemed to be always divided and mixed—pineapple-coconut or strawberry-guava or watermelon-mango. He found these brews utterly tasteless since fidelity to *one* fruit's flavour or taste had become, sadly, inconsequential.

Spotting an old-fashioned sugarcane shop tucked away at a corner, Neelkantha quickly ordered a tall glass and sat down. Before him, he could see a huge crowd slowly dispersing on the sands of Chowpatty beach.

"Minister *sahib* just left, sir. You should have been here half an hour ago," the owner of the juice stand told him sorting out the sugarcanes. "You know, there was the usual *tamasha*. These politicians *suars*. They will use any occasion to get votes. Gandhi's *charkha*, he called it. Then, pausing to get his English right, Bapu's spinning wheel. As if that motherfucker had ever spun one in his lifetime?

"Couldn't even pronounce it properly. *Iskerlator*, he called it. Now tell me *sahib*, what do we need escalators for? And at Chowpatty? These *gadhas* will always walk on the road. That's our Indian birthright. Let's see how long that damned *iskerlator* will run. It'll probably shut down in a month. *Ek mahina*. That's all I'm giving it. What do you say, sir? Shall we have a bet? It'll shut down in one month like everything else that is electrified in our glorious city."

"That will be nine rupees, sir. Sorry, sir, I don't have change for 50 rupees. What?! You want me to keep the change! Good lord! Which side did the sun rise today? Wait, sir. I shall get you your change. No, sir. Please wait. Sir? SIR? SURR?"

But the overjoyed Neelkantha was hurrying towards that *iskerlator*. Like a Chaplin shouting that he had found his "mountain of gold" at last, he rushed towards his metaphorical spot. He had, finally, found it.

"WARNING! ESCALATOR WILL BE SHUT OFF AT 12 PM. IT WILL START AT 6 A.M. CHILDREN SHOULD ALWAYS BE ACCOMPANIED BY ADULTS." How glowing that notice suddenly appeared to him. He decided to wait till midnight. Then, when Bombay prepared to sleep and with the poison safely advanced in his body, he would quietly arrange himself on this passive escalator and finally go to sleep. Yes, embrace that final sleep from which nobody awakens.

He wondered who would be the first person to find his lifeless body the next morning, or "At 6 a.m.", as the notice said. He hoped his family would not be disappointed. He imagined what Meenakshi would say: "Our dad was very unique, you know. He died publicly on an escalator." Then he imagined Jyoti stepping forward and proclaiming: "In full view of Bombay, he fenced with death, that dear mad husband of mine." Satya, as usual, would have the last word: "Thank God, he showed some imagination when he died."

Watching the stars above him in a sky emptied of all clouds, Neelkantha suddenly started laughing. And as he laughed, the phrases of his wife and his children got all mangled and were ripped apart by the awful racket that that active escalator was making as it remorselessly clock-worked itself into that final exhaustion that had been his for his entire lifetime.

WHEN STILL LIFE STILL MOVES

Fourteen more steps. Then Mummy will be right beneath the arch. It's so white, our family courtyard. There's been no wind for two days. Even the birds don't leave their nests. I can't hit Mummy with my sling-shot. That's for the birds. And I don't want grandfather to beat me again. It hurts. Just because he can't walk, he beats me so hard and that too always on my legs. Old fool. His wrists are so strong. Why doesn't Granny change his shawl and pyjamas? They always smell of castor oil and eucalyptus.

Only 12 more steps, Mummy. I'm 10 years old but Granny says I look older. Of course I do. What does that old hag know? All she does is cook, wash and pray. I'm more than 10 years old, Mummy, but you don't know. That's my secret.

Do you have one, Mummy? I'm sure you have lots of secrets hidden in that big city. Once, I heard you screaming at Granny—"He's his father's son! Call that coward. He's hiding somewhere in the mountains. He's only pretending to be a soldier."

How nice Daddy would look in a soldier's uniform. I've only seen photographs of him wrestling with some men in a pit. When I grow up, I'll become a wrestler too.

Then only I'll become a soldier. Just like Daddy. That'll show you. All *you* do is get me presents from the city. O, those foolish monkeys you brought for me last time. They used to grin at me and bang a drum. Now they won't. I broke all their springs.

When Daddy comes home, I'll ask him to teach me how to wrestle. That's much better than playing with your stupid monkeys. Ten steps, nine steps, eight steps, you're getting closer, Mummy, good, seven steps, six steps, five steps...

~

That little boy is really getting out of hand. Hé Ram. If only I could walk. Hé Ram, how my feet yearn to feel the earth again. He's growing old very quickly. This place seems to get whiter and whiter every day. Wish there was some damned wind. Now what is that rascal doing on top of the arch? Ah, it's ta ta time again and he doesn't want to be kissed by his mother. So he's climbed up there!

Mother, indeed! She has only two days in a month for us and her precious son. God only knows what other things she does in the city. She has guts, though. Must admit that, and courage. Yes, much more than what my son had—that coward! Ran away and joined the Army. Ha! If you can't live with an educated city-bred wife, join the Army. Hé Ram.

But what sins did we commit to have this shame thrust upon us, especially now in our old age? We should have checked her family background more thoroughly before arranging the match. That damned *munshi*. He was always in a hurry to get his 40 per cent commission.

But we needed the money as well from the dowry she bought. That is why we said "Yes". God, how we needed the money. Everything gets reduced to money, hé Ram, everything, everything.

And speaking about money, how much did I get from that forest contractor as "compensation"? Stupid bloody word. As though it could lift that tree after it had crushed my feet completely. I feel its weight, even today, every day.

I'm glad the boy takes after his city-bred mother. At least he'll survive even if 10 trees were to fall on him. And she does give us enough cash, every time she comes here, to make two square meals over the stove. I don't grudge her that. How can I? She's well educated and she's…also…very beautiful. And how she makes us understand that, the cunning witch.

We're dependent on her. That is why we cannot openly tell her anything. If only I could walk. I'd show her. I'd really show her what my son couldn't. But she's so beautiful. So...so...beautiful...

~

Look at that slut! Tying her sari so low once again. And her blouses? They seem to get tinier and tinier and seem to shrink with every visit. Must be for the benefit of all those young strapping farmers' sons going to the fields to work. Why, that cunning temple-dancer! If she had her way, she'd corrupt even those thin but earnest young school boys cycling, for her benefit, so slowly as they pass by our house. She was born to make all mens' palms wet. And we had to go and marry our son to this, this, defilement!

She likes teasing the old man too. I can see the longing in his eyes and the froth around his lips. It's been years since he looked like that at another woman. Me? O, he stopped looking at me years ago. And how she drove my son mad as well. *Parmatma*, may her son give her exactly what she gave mine.

That damn tree. It didn't fall *only* on his legs. I wish it had fallen on her when they were going around the sacred fire. We had spread so many colours that day in this courtyard. "Too much of whiteness is not very auspicious, Mother," the astrologer had told me. "Sprinkle some colours in the courtyard." So I did. I did. But he had kept quiet. O, what a fool I was. I was so blinded by happiness. I should have guessed. But why didn't that wise man warn me? Why did he keep silent about the future? He could have at least given me some hint, any hint?

O, what's the use. You can't wring dirty water out of a destiny like this, this washed sari! It's all HIS will!

"Hé you! Get down from that arch before you fall down. Get down. You hear. Get down, you monkey."

Ram, Ram, when will all this end...when...when...

~

I come here for two days and all they do is *watch* me—like an insect, like a worm. Dear Father. Mother. I hope YOU are happy in your damn city. Daughters are only guaranteers for their parents' retirement benefits. Right? Then what was the point in *educating* me if I was to be singled out to marry a dull clod of a wrestler? I hope you will be doing penance for me when next you go to

Benares. And don't bring back any holy *gangajal* for me. I have washed away all my purity.

And I mustn't forget to thank you for the good *looks* which I inherited from both of you as well. I'm using *them* to keep *these* three alive. The boy is too young to understand. I have to win him over slowly. You should see him. He circles around me like a wrestler every time I come here. Watching me and waiting. What is he waiting for? He even wrestled with me in my womb, prolonging the labour. Remember?

Men have it so easy, so damned easy, compared to us womenfolk. O, these fancy city men with all their swagger and their continuous loud talk. Strip them bare and they tremble. Nakedness makes them uneasy. How I love that power. It makes me, in that one tiny moment, obliterate the whole bloody bundle—parents, in-laws, husband, wife, children. And it's nice to make them cling, make them beg. O Lord, *how* I make them beg when I take them to the top and...and...yes, it's true. *I* don't feel a thing. So what if I *pretend* all the time that I do. I have that other 9 to 5 job. That makes one feel decent enough. Once that one stops, this one begins. Why make all this fuss? But what is he doing on the arch? Challenging me? Again?

~

Ten steps, nine, eight steps, you're getting closer, Mummy... seven steps, six, five steps...

~

What is he counting? How tall and handsome he looks. Ah, the old man has started frothing at his lips again.

What a big role I must be playing in his dried up dreams. God. There's too much sun here, too much glare. No tree in sight. How beautiful the courtyard had looked on my wedding day. Vibrant with colour. So much colour and...

~

Hey, you! Get down from that arch before you fall. Get down. You hear. Get down, you monkey...

Poor thing. Look at her. Menopause always comes early to us Indian women. I guess one day it will come to me too. I can already feel the dryness in my womb. And yet she's so devoted, so dutiful. But doesn't she know what I'm going through? Isn't she a woman too? I guess, unlike me, she was determined to be only obedient and ordinary. But that's the way Indian men want us.

O darling son of mine. How strong you look on that arch. I wonder what your father looks like standing guard on a remote mountain peak and staring at an invisible enemy. I tried to make him a man, my son. I tried, honestly, I did, to make him see himself, for once, outside his accepted roles of son and husband. But I failed. All he ever understood and memorised was only the wrestler's art. I'm glad you're not like him. I think you take after me. Someday you'll understand me. Then you'll hold me close. Call me "Mother" instead of "city-*bai*". I'll wait for that day, my son, I'll wait...

~

And then the little boy spread his legs and pissed on his mother. White glistening urine fell in a steady arc on her drained, stupefied face. A spring inside her seemed to snap. But she stood there like a soldier, erect, lifeless, bathing in it as though it was just another version of *gangajal*.

The froth around the old man's lips dripped slowly down to his lap. White, glistening and warm, it formed a large puddle around his loins.

The old woman clutched the wet sari to her heart and slowly hid her face in it. Was she laughing? Crying?

It is difficult to tell, when still life still moves.

HIS OMELETTE AND HER *TANDAVA*

Anuja looked at Siva's face in the car's rear view mirror. It glowed as usual with confidence. Her fingers lovingly fondled the expensive gift she had bought for him. It lay beside her, neatly wrapped in brown paper. She knew he hated glossy gift-wrap paper.

His wife and kids had left suddenly for Calcutta. He was taking her to his flat for the weekend for the first time. No wife. No kids. Just the two of them. How well he drove the car. She watched his fingers on the steering wheel. He always seemed to have everything under control.

A few years ago, they had met at a party. And what a new world he had opened up for her. All those dull and drab academic historians whom she had to tolerate during her boring afternoon lectures at the university became live dramatic characters when *he* expounded on the same subjects every evening, in her room.

He was twice her 20 years but always treated her as an "exciting equal"! She was proud of that definition he had imposed on her. It helped, at least, in momentarily rebuking the hooded demons that lashed out at her. But over a period of time they had become second nature as she had proverbially slipped into the role of that *other* woman!

She looked at the contours of his face once again, to detect some kind of trembling, a glimpse of vulnerability, and finding none once again, she decided that she couldn't care less. Which girl of a mere 20 wouldn't be flattered by the persistent attentions of the well-known Siva Saxena?

She leaned forward and fondled his hair. He had asked her to sit behind him "just as a precaution", especially at traffic lights where someone familiar could cross the road and cast that puzzled look at them. She smiled and fondled his hair once again. There was a faint smell of fish that day in the breeze that was blowing in persistently from the sea.

Suddenly, he slammed the brakes. Anuja was thrown rudely against her gift. In an effort to hold on to something, four of her fingers tore right through the gift-packing and clumsily grasped a solid bronze arch. Why did she always avoid using the car's seat belts?

A legless beggar on a large skating-board suddenly darted across the road. As Anuja regained her balance, she caught a quick glimpse of contempt curl itself, like a whip, around Siva's mouth. "Damned beggars," he muttered fiercely. "They thrive on charity and now they want to become martyrs under my car. Are you all right, my love?"

She smiled and fell back against the seat. What a pity, the brown paper was torn. They drove on in silence. And then for no reason at all, that word 'martyr' which he had so casually uttered suddenly started to move like a windshield wiper across her thoughts. She looked at Siva's face again. It was calm and emotionless as always. What was he planning now? The usual seduction after he had foreplayed her first with that particular symphony which he would put on "exclusively for you" on the turntable? Followed by why it was written and for whom it was played and how the first movement flowed into the second? And the third? Till it crescendoed and reached a climax?

This time, however, it was *all* to be at *his* house. Now that indeed was a first. She knew there was a first time for everything, but she shuddered at the idea of actually making love in the same bed where his wife and he slept every night. She had always wanted to know 'a little more' about his wife, Parul. But he seemed to dismiss her every time with the same remark, "I like her and I respect her, Anuja. But it is you I love and it is you I want. So don't break your pretty little head or your prettier little body over *her*."

But wasn't it just *her* pretty little head and *her* prettier little body which was being so regularly broken?

"Now, my love, listen to me." With a start, Anuja ejected herself from her geared-up thoughts. "I'll drop you at the corner and I'll go ahead and park the car in the garage. I'm on the eleventh floor. Don't enquire and don't pretend to scan the names in the lobby. Just walk right up to the lift. I'll enter five minutes after you. We'll go up together. You ask the liftman to take you to the 15th floor. I'll get off at the 11th. We won't say a word. You get off on the 15th. Wait for the lift to go down first. Then come down the stairs quickly. Don't ring the bell. I'll keep the door slightly open. Take the gift with you. It'll make you look more hospitable. This liftman, unlike yours, is quite a gossipy character. Like my driver. Damned peasants. They love biting the hand that feeds them. And they say the rich exploit the poor in India!"

Her fingers held on to that bronzed arch inside the torn packet. All these manipulations, all these instructions, how she had come to steadily hate them! Why couldn't he ever be *proud* of their relationship? Had it not stood some test of time? Then why this daily *tamasha*? Who is *he* to talk about martyrs anyway? He is so far removed, so…so…distant from any of them.

Didn't he realise that she was also someone's daughter causing her old parents a lot of pain every time he came over to *her* flat, made her lock her bedroom door, so that they could make love between his two morning conferences and her two afternoon postgraduate History classes? How could she crescendo and climax while downstairs his two little girls played in the car with a chuckling driver, waiting for their "Daddy" to finally "come" down and take them for a walk as the horses were being put through their paces at the Mahalakshmi race course?

She smiled. She loved him, just as his wife Parul did, and she needed him, just as his kids did. She looked at his face again as he finally stopped the car. He was exactly like the bronze statue of God Siva wrapped up in that packet. She sighed. Love affairs are easy to deal with when they are always wrapped up. What happens, what happens, she wondered, when the wrappings finally come off?

Half an hour later, she felt calm again. They had unwrapped her gift and she watched him place it proudly on the writing desk in his study. "How will you explain this gift to Parul?" Anuja suddenly asked him. But he had not even heard her. He was scrutinising the statue with such excitement that she felt she had spoken out of turn. In the expensive *khadi bhandar* she had looked with adoration at this bronze Siva. Now she suddenly felt a surging hatred, especially at that celebrated dance of the *tandava* that both these Sivas were performing for her benefit.

"...it means, Anuja, the dance of destruction. After Siva has destroyed the world, and," he chuckled, "people like *us*, for all our splendidly calculated sins, he dances this *tandava*. You see this little drum he is holding in one of his hands? It is called a *dumroo*. By shaking it, he intends to create a new world. A purer world, an ethical world, where everyone loves everyone else sincerely...very different from our present one, mind you. And this metal bronze arch behind his head with all these little flames of fire flickering in them stands for our world which is burning, burning. And *that* is the small, ugly dwarf of ignorance and conventions that he is crushing with his other foot. Have you read..."

"What will you tell Parul when she asks you who gave you this gift?" Anuja repeated the question, a little fiercely this time.

"I'll tell her I bought it at one of those quaint *raddi purana* shops at Chor Bazaar. She knows I go there often. Remind me to take you there next week. Come on. Don't look so cheerless. Why don't you go and relax in the hall while I make you that Spanish omelette as I promised? When I was at Harvard, I learnt how to make it, but don't ask me from whom. Okay? Now be a good girl. Up you go."

Anuja looked at the statue again. How could such a cultured and intelligent man invent lies so glibly about it, and place it on his desk, look at it every day, lecture about it, without ever trying to give it, even once, any kind of precious validity? She wished she had not bought it. In the shop it had looked so majestic. Even its weight had somehow impressed her. But now it weighed on her differently. She felt humiliated, crushed, almost like that dwarf, trodden by this other Siva, who was now busy in the kitchen nonchalantly creating a Spanish omelette that he had learnt from...was it so hard to guess?

She dreaded going into the bedroom. There were so many clues about his "home" and his "marriage", right here in the hall. On several occasions, she had longed to pick up the phone and proudly proclaim over the mouthpiece to Mrs. Parul Saxena that she, Miss Anuja Desai, was her husband's real love! But she had never had the courage to do that.

Now she was in *her* house and in *her* hall. A sudden desire to imagine this 'other' woman, this wife whom he rarely talked about, now took hold of her. Parul *had* to be unique in some way, otherwise he would have left her a long time ago. But he hadn't. He had always insisted that he *liked* her, *respected* her, *and* that he would *never* leave her. When she had demanded why, he had just irritably answered, "We never quarrel. We have no problems. We have—what is the word—adjusted. What she learnt from her parents, she practises. One word sums it up—duty. And duty, my darling, always takes care of love."

This conversation had occurred in the middle of an open-air Indian classical music concert at two in the morning. There had been an impromptu hush in the musical proceedings, as a screaming fire-engine, rushing by, had disturbed the concentration of one of the singing *ustads*. Those words had fallen like heavy descending notes from his mouth. "Duty, my darling, always takes care of love." How desperately she had wanted that fire engine to return and forcibly ruin that concert. But it had gone raging into the dawn to put out another fire, somewhere, in another part of the city, ignoring hers completely.

On the recording cabinet were a number of long playing records, haphazardly piled up. Every record sleeve bore the name "Parul". The handwriting was a childish scrawl that brought on a sudden twisted smile, like a leash, to Anuja's face. There were the usual wedding photographs on the wall. They seemed, very strangely, to have something defiant about them. No matter how hard she tried to analyse Parul's physical features as the camera had caught them, Anuja still couldn't find any fault with them. How pretty she looked. How confident. How, how, what was that word, *centred*!

"Is Parul still as pretty as she was on your marriage day?" she suddenly inquired.

"That, my dear, is the privilege of the wealthy," he replied from the kitchen. "People who are neat and tidy and who don't think too much somehow seem to retain much more of their beauty than the untidy ones, the visionaries, the risk-takers, like you and I," he remarked artfully, winking at her.

"I see. Well, the next time when you come to my untidy room, Siva darling, I'll make you actually straighten out all the mess. Especially the new ones that you continue to give me with every new risk you force me to take."

There was a burst of laughter from the kitchen, followed by a yelp of pain. "Ouch. I nearly martyred myself for your Spanish omelette."

Ugh! That dreadful word again. She wondered if this print of Picasso's had also been a present given to him. Yes. She was right. It was. There was Parul's childish scrawl in the corner again. She noticed though, that she had somehow misspelt the word "*anniversary*". It appeared to her as *adversary*. Now that seemed to delight her. Then her eyes wandered lazily between the Siva statue and the Picasso print.

"Did you give your wife a long lecture when she gave you this Picasso print? And did you talk about his Blue Periods and the bombs falling on Guernica and his endless stream of mistresses?"

"What's the matter with you, Anuja?" How refined he looked, even with the frying pan in his hand and the cooking apron across his waist. "No, my dear, I didn't. I merely kissed her and said a heartfelt, mind you, only a heartfelt 'Thank you'. For your present, though, you will receive much more, but first you have to taste my Spanish omelette."

She thought that vulgar, so she walked past him into the kitchen. "Hmm, I expected your kitchen to be neat. That's where a wife really leaves her 'stamp,' you know. But those tiles do look a little grimy round the edges, don't they? She should supervise your Gurkha *khansama* more sternly. People who don't think much are quite neat and orderly, did you say? Your wife then seems to be a notable exception. She..."

"Look. Let's stop this charade, shall we? Now come and eat your omelette like a good girl. I've slaved so lovingly over it."

"I don't want to eat your damn omelette. And don't talk to me about being a slave!"

"Anuja! What's the matter with you? Look, come and lie down. I'll pull the shades. You'll get a wonderful view of the sea. It's very soothing to look at the sea, especially when one is stressed. Try it. We...we do it all the time."

It *was* a wonderful view of the sea. Waves of embarrassment at her own sudden viciousness swept over her. He lay beside her, softly stroking her hair. As usual, he began lecturing. He was saying something about "Conrad," and his obsession with "the sea". Then she vaguely heard "Hemingway" and "Cuba" added to the list, but her mind had begun to wander far away from them, from the sea, even from that damn omelette. Her eyes were darting all over the bedroom like a lizard in search of its victim.

The closet drawers were half open. He had said, "She had left in a hurry" to catch the morning flight to Calcutta. The strap of a brassiere, several crumpled underwear, and a panty hose were stuffed untidily in them. She was desperately looking for some remnants of neatness. On the dressing table, a number of lipsticks lay half open. There was a smear of rouge on one of the drawer handles. Hurriedly folded blankets had been clumsily squeezed under the mattress. As she turned her head, the smell of an expensive shampoo leaked into her nostrils from one of the pillow covers. She jumped up suddenly. Just then, the phone started to ring.

"What's the matter, darling? What's bothering you? Hold on. Hold on. Let me answer the—

"Hello? Parul? Yes, this *is* a surprise! But I thought you were going to come back on Monday. I see. Where are you, at the airport? Okay. I'll send the car. Wait for it. No. No. Please don't take a cab. No honey, I can't come. I have this meeting to prepare for tomorrow. Yes, I'll send Ram Mohan. How are the kids? Tell them Daddy is waiting. Come soon."

He put the phone down and dialled the garage number. He gave instructions to Ram Mohan to proceed to the airport and pick up Memsaab and the kids.

"I'm taking my gift with me." Anuja had picked up the Siva statue. Cradling it in her arms, she said, "I'll think of an inconspicuous gift next time. Something that your untidy wife will miss out on."

He put down the phone and went towards her.

"Now don't be silly, Anuja. Just leave it here. Look, I'm sorry, but I'll drop you home. Come, give me that other Siva now. And stop behaving like a little girl."

"Don't touch me, Siva. Please. I said, don't touch me. Will you stop grabbing that damn statue? If you like it so much then take it, damn it, take it, TAKE IT, TAKE IT…"

"No Anuja, no..." He held her tightly as she collapsed in his *tandava*-like arms. She would have liked to slam the door on his face, or better still, to hurl that Siva statue right through the window into the sea. But she just stood there sobbing. He was talking to her gently, soothing her... calming her down, like the sea which she could see in the distance. She had become like a statue that he was slowly bringing back to life again so that the other dance could once again be performed. He started it by picking up the car keys. She knew what she had to do. He had trained her so well. Go to the 15th floor. He would join her on the 11th. She would walk to the corner. Wait for the cab. Quietly open the back door. Get in. And await further instructions.

THE DANCE LESSON

The noise of the dancing anklets woke Salma up. "Dance! Dance properly, you whore! Dance!" Was it in a dream she was hearing those words? How ugly they sounded, especially in Urdu. Someone dropped anklets in the next room. There was a muffled giggle. But Urdu was such a soft and dulcet language. It reminded her of sparkling fountains and silken bed covers and wine being slowly poured into silver tumblers and men in exquisite clothes reciting well-rehearsed couplets in hushed voices to their women as they applied paint delicately to their freshly cut toenails. Here, all she got were *gaali*s. Why didn't they utter such profanities in their Bombaia-Hindustani? All men were *suar*s anyway. Her back really hurt. First they tired you on your feet by making you dance. Then they penetrated you with quick thrusts of their lust. And afterwards they abused you in all sorts of ways (since it came with the price) so that they could feel masculine all over again before they left for their damned respectable homes and their weak spineless wives.

Over here everything was negotiated in the name of *honour*. How nice that word sounded in Urdu. It was, as Ammi-jaan said, a *sawal*, a question of *"izzat"*. *Hai Allah!*

Who was banging the tabla so inexpertly and trying to keep time with those damned anklets in the next room?

Salma dragged herself out of bed. The sun, aiming a sudden point of light through the wooden shutters, expertly shot at her eyes. She sat down on the bed again, closing her eyes tightly. If it was the sun in the day, it was the tobacco at night, especially the smoke that made her eyes smart. "Payal," she suddenly shouted, as she lay back against the pillows. "Payal, come to *amma* now. Come here instantly."

That child was really getting out of hand. Suddenly Salma smiled as she recalled the day Payal was born. What argument there had been amongst the regular clients as to what they should call "our" Salma's child. Each thought, secretly of course, that one of them was the actual father. So each felt he was entitled to suggest a name for their imagined daughter. It was Usmaan, the *paanwala*, who had come up with "Payal". Since Ammi-jaan had liked that name, it had stuck.

"She will dance like her mother," Ammi-jaan had told Salma as she had taken the wailing baby in her arms and softly kissed her. "Since her name means 'anklet', she'll have no difficulty in wearing her first pair, will she, Salma? I hope she grows up quickly so I can give her her first dance lesson. I'm growing old now. I won't be around now. I want *her* to be my last creation. Maybe my best creation." She had looked at the baby, and then had suddenly taken her tiny fingers and placed them on her forehead. "Bless me, my child. Bless me for the future I am already planning for you. We are merely dancers who spread a lot of *sangeet* and a lot of *mithaas* for the very frightened people of the world. Ah, they boast a lot, but they are really very frightened, my child. That is why they come to *us*! So you see. There is pride, my little one, in what we do. The world may find us wanting in music and in our *aurat pesha*. But we don't. I hope you'll remember that."

At last Payal came shyly into the room. She had smeared her face with a ghastly white chalk and had applied dark *kajal* all around her large saucer eyes. She was even chewing *paan* to look like her mother—an authentic *tawaif*, a *naachnevali*. For Payal, Salma, indeed, was the best. There was no one like her. Of course, her mother's anklets were too big for her now but she had tried to wrap them round her small legs with more than one rag that she had somehow managed to find. As she walked towards her mother, she deliberately swung her hips, trying to mimic Salma's tantalising gait which had been such a hit with her customers.

The slap was hard and tight and it caught Payal right in the middle of her last titillating step towards her mother. "Don't you cry. Not one word. Not one tear. You horrible child. Aren't you ashamed of yourself, putting on all that stuff, and where did you learn to walk like that? You think that makes me proud? You think all that I do, I like doing? You think so? You think so? You little minx. You li—"

"Stop frightening Payal. She's too young to understand your rants. And don't you dare raise your hand on a mere child while her Ammi-jaan is still alive. Now, Payal, come to Ammi-jaan. There, there. Did your Amma slap you very hard? She did? Go put your face under the tap and wash away all that powder and *kajal*. I'll teach you how to apply them properly. I've made some *gajar-halwa* for you. It's getting heated in the kitchen. Go and eat it and then come to my room. I'll tell you a story. Run now. I want to talk to your Amma. Come on. Brave girls don't cry. That's my little *rani*."

Payal stopped sniffing and took off her anklets. Then flinging them angrily at Salma, she ran out of the room.

"You did that to me too, Salma, the very first day you were brought here. Do you remember? It was a heavy *payal*, my child. It hit me right here, near the belly button. There, do you see that scar? Yet I never slapped you, did I? In this house, only customers are allowed to slap us. Not us, my child. Never us," Ammi-jaan reminded Salma.

"That's what I hate about our country, Ammi-jaan. That's what is so rotten here." Salma's eyes flashed angrily as she picked up the anklets and placed them beside the small *gajra* lying on the bedside table. For a long time, she said nothing. She kept staring at the exquisite *gajra*s men wore round their wrists when they courted whores like her. She wondered why they never did that with their own wives. This one was Usmaan's. He was the most decent of the lot. He always soothed her before emptying out his day's tiredness inside her. He even lit her favourite *agarbatti*s for her in the room before leaving. "Why are we *tawaifs* so looked down upon?" she asked Ammi-jaan as she bent down to light a fresh *agarbatti*. "Are we not romanticised in poetry, and wooed in *ghazal*s? Why, even in the Hindi films, respected actresses long to play the roles of *tawaifs*. But not in life, of course. No, never in life. That is why, *Ammi-jaan*, I don't want Payal to be what I am. I want her to—"

"Child. Stop your wishful thinking. This is our *naseeb*. Listen to me. Take the words *'bhen'* or 'Ammi-jaan'. One means 'sister'. The other means 'mother'. When I get into a crowded bus and a stranger gets up and offers me his seat, he always says, '*Ma*, please sit here.' Now, if it was you instead of me, he would address you as *'bhen.'* Yet when that same man has a quarrel with another and gives him all those terrible *gaalis*, its always the "mother" and "sister" who are targeted in those *gaalis*. What we hear is always 'I'll fuck your *sister*' or 'May your *mother's* private parts be burnt.' The funny thing is that even when *women* abuse each other, they say the same thing! Imagine? I've even heard those *gaalis* from *your* own mouth, Salma, and even *I* am guilty of *ma-bhen* abuses like that."

"I do not dispute your wisdom, Ammi-jaan. You have been both mother and grandmother to me. And you have been much more than that to my little girl. But I don't, I don't want *her* to follow in my footsteps. Let her get a good education. Let her go away from here. I don't care if she doesn't come even to see me. Let her, let her at least—" Tears of anger and guilt and shame streamed down Salma's face.

Ammi-jaan recognised them as she bent down to wipe them away with her arthritic fingers. Both women knew that tears like these rarely wash away anything.

"Do you want Payal to go away like Maqbool, Usmaan's son? You remember Maqbool, don't you? Why he even broke a man's jaw once in the *mohalla* to preserve your *tawaif izzat*. You should have seen the way he stormed out of our house when he came to know that you had also entertained his father in the same manner as you entertained him. Ah, these men. All their egos lie below their waists."

"He never came back, did he, Ammi-jaan? I was told that that same night he left his father's house and—"

"And it is Usmaan who now goes to visit him, especially on Ramzaan. Maqbool has become a very respectable man since then, my child. He is a *bangla-gaadi* man now. He can spare only half an hour for his old father. He has a lovely wife and two very obedient children. Do you know what they call their grandfather? *'Chacha.'* And why? Because he's embarrassed and ashamed of having a father who plies his trade as an ordinary *paanwala*. Especially in a red-light area like ours. Do you want your Payal to become another Maqbool? Do you?"

Salma didn't say anything. She shyly touched *Ammi*-jaan's feet with her fingers and then put them to her lips. Then she quickly walked past the old woman to the bathroom. Opening the tap, she put her face to the cold gushing water. It seemed to cool the sting of the slap she had just delivered on her daughter's face. As she washed her face with soap, she was surprised at the scent of the *agarbattis* still lingering on her fingers as she looked at her face in the mirror. She waited. Then she slowly smiled at the woman in the mirror. Today, she would not try to wash away the *paan*-stains from her teeth. That would make Usmaan really happy.

When she went back to her bed, Ammi-jaan was gone. But there was a pair of brand new anklets placed on the centre of the bed. Salma picked them up and smiled. Quietly closing her bed-room door, she went to

Ammi-jaan's chamber. Normally, she would have knocked. But today, the door was half open.

Slowly easing the door a little more, she thrust the anklets through the gap and shook them. The peal of the little bells made Ammi-jaan and little Payal turn their heads towards the sound. For a fraction of an eternity, those tinkling bells joined the two beings inside the room to the one outside it.

"Payal," said Salma, hidden behind the door," your dance lessons will begin from tomorrow."

PESTONJI'S TOWER OF SILENCE

Pestonji paused at the second turn of the *kasti*. God had been all along behind him when he was a young man. O, that rascal! He had pushed him into everything. He had not even been allowed to dream. As he finished his prayers, he suddenly started thinking about those stairs. God, how he hated climbing them. But he did. Just to defy them: daily to his office, then daily to his house. One day they had had their revenge by suddenly making him feel old and breathless. Just like that. Growing old had come to him as an epiphany surprising him in mid-stride. But on the day he retired, he curiously missed those stairs. And now God seemed always to stand above him. But he was in no hurry to push himself towards God. No Sir. Like a good gentleman, God would have to wait for him. But that tower of silence, looming always behind God, continued to nag him. He was not afraid of vultures. But the thought of his naked body on that wooden plank, inviting those damned birds to actually have a feast, suddenly made him very angry. Why hadn't the prophet of his religion devised another way, a less messier one, of leaving this world?

"Granddad, will you tie my school-tie, please?"

Hastily tying all his prayers behind his back in a knot, Pestonji's fingers grudgingly completed for his granddaughter a tiny but 'propah' Windsor knot.

"There!" he said. "That was one subtlety the Britishers taught us. And thank God for that."

"What does 'subtlety' mean, Granddad?"

"That is a word, my dear, you'll understand only when you're grown up. Don't let anybody explain it to you, especially now. Run along now, and see you next Friday. Give my love to Mummy and Daddy. Here. Let me see your tie again. Ah! Perfect." He waited for little Maharuk to leave the room, before he turned round and mockingly bowed to the portraits of the Royal Family. Alamai, his wife, had arranged them all on one wall of their bedroom. How cunningly had she set an entire *gora* hierarchy up there besides their own families' portraits, assembled obediently under them.

But why did she call me "Granddad" instead of our very own Parsi word, *"Bappa-va-jee"*? It meant the same thing, of course, but it sounded so much nicer, more intimate, especially on one's tongue. It's all the fault of these bloody convent schools. She knows the names of all those prophets in the Old Testament, but all our Parsi zealots remain complete strangers to her. And it's degrading for me to point *them* out to her as dirty statues shivering out there in the rain or sweating it out in Byculla's Victoria Garden Zoo. This bloody municipality should be horsewhipped. They bathe their revered saints with milk and offer *prasad* to them in their temples and leave ours to the shit and piss of crows and other birds.

Tying the knot of his pyjamas fastidiously for the fifth time, Pestonji finally settled down in his ancestral easy chair. An empty teacup stood on the small table beside him. He stirred a solitary spoon in it. The cup's rim was broad enough and it reminded him constantly of that well inside the tower of silence. On that day, the vultures will sit on it. First, one vulture will come and eye my naked body lying there. Like this solitary spoon. What can I offer God then? As a corpse, I shall be completely stripped, both of my *ahura* and of my *mazda*. I will just lie there, like a mock pharaoh, slowly to become a bundle of bloody flesh slowly masticated in one enormous scavenging beak after another. No fuss of embalming here. All those *shakahari*s would applaud, wouldn't they? It would be poetic justice that a *masahari* would meet his end between the powerful jaws of a bird that didn't care one way or the other! He closed his eyes for a moment and felt the brush of a scraggy wing.

And, then, slowly but determinedly, within the depths of both his closed eyes, arose, once again the gradually forming vision of his entire caste, standing as one man, and doing some kind of a tedious and monotonous physical drill, there, over there, in the distance, but near, very near, that damn tower.

But what about Kekashroo, my pet cockatoo? That bird always seemed to bring him back from the tower. *Now* the bugger was silent. But on *that* fateful day would he be silent? Birds have a way of sniffing out death. *I* had known that even before reading my Shakespeare. And my Kekashroo, my dear, dear Kekashroo, is not even a vulture. Still, he would pierce the bars of the cage with shrill screams for his daily dose of breadcrumbs. Somebody would feed him eventually, I guess, but how could anyone explain the absence of its regular master to a bird that had insisted on his presence every single day and every single night, now for so many years...so many years...

I shall not come on that day my darling bird. Those vultures won't let me. And I'm not just referring only to birds. Look at the money they will spend on that day over all the isus and all the sandalwood to be burnt over my departed flesh before the birds chewed it all up. Prayers would have to be paid for, too. God is an expensive master and our masked priests, our rascal *dasturjis*, are like those *Mujhe Jeene Do* dacoits, always demanding a tidy sum *before* agreeing to chant all their Chambal-rehearsed litanies. Ah, those *badmashes*? They only know how to gargle before the sacred *atash* in their ag..., no...no...their *ugh yarees*.

Come, come, my moppet. Take some breadcrumbs now. I bought them especially for you from old Gustaadji's bakery. Poor man. Once he was so proud of baking his breads, all so meticulously, especially the *brun* that came piping out from his ovens twice a day. He had four ovens and three sons. Did you know that? Now, all his sons have left for America and he has no one left even to heat one oven or make a dozen bread loaves. So, dear bird, he is now reduced to selling only breadcrumbs. I, at least, am lucky. I have you and my Alamai, and my children, and little Maharuk, of course.

The smell of freshly fried *popatjis* and freshly baked *bhakrahs* drifted in from the kitchen. It seemed to drive away all vultures and breadcrumbs from Pestonji's mind. After all these years, her *jadoo* had still not evaporated from that accustomed smell. Dear, beloved Alamai. In the darkness of the Metro theatre he had proposed to her, as a young man of 18. In those days, we married young, Kekashroo. I had taken her to see *Waterloo Bridge*. And just when Robert Taylor kissed Vivian Leigh, I had leaned close to her in the dark, and had asked her to marry me! And she had immediately said "YES." O—that small delightful word. You know, my moppet, I have always liked the Christians for murmuring "I do" in church.

Ah, I had always been a sentimentalist. But what is wrong with feelings anyway? There always seems to be a conspiracy against feelings, birdy, especially these days. But, how bold, how firm, my Alamai had been. I remember, Kekashroo, how we had stumbled out of Metro theatre. It had been drizzling, and Alamai had suggested that we go out and deliberately get wet. Daddy had just sent me my new tweeds from London, but what the dickens! We did get wet. And she, in her silk blouse and sari! We didn't care. We were so…so…happy. We ran across Azad Maidan and took refuge under the statued eyes of our Phirozshah Mehta. Yes, right there, across from Victoria Terminus station. That's why we called our son Phiroze. If we had had a daughter, we would definitely have called her Victoria! Maharuk? Is that a name? Sounds like some kind of a walnut!

Shh, there she comes, Kekashroo, still a well-oiled machine at 75. Look at the way she arranges on Grandpuppa's marble table all the silver parade of our regularly polished knives and forks. No Indian *chamcha kaatas*, these! We had bought them in Edinburgh. And you know what? Let it be our secret. It seems to add, especially these days, the taste of a forgotten British Empire. Yes, right here in my mouth. Yes, Kekashroo. This poor, sad mouth of mine, now so full of badly cemented Indian dentures.

Kekashroo plumed his feathers and clucked an encore, rolling a crumb expertly in his beak. Through one eye he watched the old man pad across the room to his old phonograph. Even the bird had become quite familiar with his routine. After whirling his right arm through 72 revolutions per minute, Al Jolson's "Jazz Singer" once again "mammy-ed" itself across the room. He came back and with all his 76 years still zestfully in motion, sat down to joyously eat his *popatjis* and *bhakrahs*. A beaming Alamai, frying spoon in hand, looked at him, even now after all these years, lovingly. He seemed to be completely lost in the miracle her cooking was once again producing on the dining table. After a while, she retreated quietly into the kitchen. A crumb cracked in the brass cage. The bird tensed because on the last groove of the song, the record needle had got stuck, once again. That never happened before. But now it was frequent. It sounded like the song's back being audibly and repeatedly broken.

Pestonji heard it too. His Master's Voice was beckoning him now to the other side of the Universe. It had been beckoning him for quite some time now. Would death come to him suddenly when he was eating Alamai's *popatjis* and *bhakrahs*? Or would it surprise him while he was feeding breadcrumbs to his lovely Kekashroo or while he was trying to tie his pyjama cords? That would be so humiliating? That vulture on the empty cup never seemed to change its size.

Suddenly he hit the cup hard with the spoon. And the vulture flew away. But it would come back tomorrow. Let it. I won't budge from behind my *machhardani*. Filthy bird. How dare it trespass every day into my house. I shall not feed you and I shall not be fodder. You hear! You won't get one crumb out of me as long as the marrow in my bones still makes me walk across the room. Now, why is Kekashroo screeching? The bird's getting old like me. I'm coming, you old fool. I'm coming.

Breaking his future, and what little was left of it now, Pestonji went slowly towards that persistent cage and that impatient bird. From far away, he could hear the football roar from the Cooperage Stadium nearby. All the Goan cooks with their Sunday-school sweethearts must have gone today to cheer their team—the Vascos. How marvellous that collective roar sounded. Why, it could frighten even that vulture away.

He waited tensely for another roar. And when it came, he let it spill slowly, lovingly, all over the room.

SAYS TRIVIKARMA, "IT'S ALL A QUESTION OF HEIGHT"

They said they would be coming at 3 p.m. That way, their entry into Bali Apartments would be inconspicuous. Most of the affluent members of this housing society would be taking their afternoon siesta or, as usual, watching MTV. The servants, the chief gossipmongers, would also be sent away on domestic errands. Three p.m. was the time they were usually dispatched by their mistresses to get fresh bread or fresh fish or fresh mutton or fresh fruit, whichever arrived first at the market, the bakery, or at the local grocers. Besides, Kersi did not want that young man called Trivikarma to create another *tamasha* as he had outside the fire-temple the day Behramsa, his father, had expired.

Kersi's normal laid-back routine had been rudely shaken, not only by his father's untimely demise, but more so by Trivikarma's loud and strange assertion that he was actually Kersi's younger brother and so had a right to be legitimately present at the *dungarwadi*. Fortunately, Jal Uncle, who was also their family lawyer, had quickly intervened. But after that shocking disclosure from a complete stranger, Kersi had not been able to concentrate on the ensuing prayers falling like heavy stones on his father's *sadrakasti* as it lay mutely on the marble slab in the *bungli*.

Kersi had never been close to his father. He hardly remembered his mother since she had died while giving birth to him. It was Janakibai, really, who had brought him up. And that had made it all the more painful. She had stood beside her real son Trivikarma and had said absolutely nothing when he had started making that painful scene.

Kersi had been a sickly boy most of his young life. Chicken-pox, small-pox, measles, typhoid, cholera, jaundice, he had gone through all historically recorded medical ailments. But the one face that he remembered sitting constantly by his bedside nursing him through *all* these illnesses had been Janakibai's.

It was, in fact, because of his frequent illnesses that his absurd video obsession had started. His father, in order to amuse and distract a territorially sick homebound lonely child, had presented him with his first TV and video monitor when he had been laid low with jaundice. And Kersi had been hooked ever since. As his sedentary life advanced, he had asked for more advanced machines and his father had duly complied. He remembered overhearing his father's words to Jal Uncle when the latter, one day, had protested about the peculiar life Kersi was leading always locked up in his room, always indoors, and always before his 30 TVs and video machines.

"What education-feducation are you talking about, Jal? I have made enough money in the Shipping Corporation and the Share Bazar to last three generations. I have invested all of it in Kersi's name. After I am gone, he can live off all my investments. He doesn't need a regular job. He doesn't even have to stir out of the house. And as our family lawyer, you jolly well see to that. *Lagan-bagan* also is out of the question for our *bayloo* Kersi. Besides, that boy won't ever amount to anything. Just leave him to his TVs and videos. At least he has one passion."

"Ah, but Trivikarma, now that's what I called you here to talk about. Come into my study. He is doing very well, you know, after I enrolled him in the J.J. School of Architecture. Why, just the other day I received a call from the Dean..."

At that moment Janakibai had arrived with his medicine. It was strange how his memory had suddenly rewound to that very scene when one of the *agyari* priests had rushed up to Kersi and whispered to him that a young servant *chhokra* and a *gangabai* were creating a lot of commotion outside the *agyari*'s entrance. Not wanting his father's final rites to be rudely desecrated like this, Kersi had quickly walked outside, followed by the ever vigilant Jal Uncle.

That was the first time Kersi had ever laid eyes on Trivikarma. He was very short and surprisingly fair. But what shocked Kersi was the same high forehead, the same light brown eyes, the same aquiline nose, and the same cruel mouth of his father, his *father*, now suddenly etched on this, on this *chhokra*'s face that was shouting abuses at him.

"These *sala mobeds* won't let us in, Kersi *seth*. We may not be Parsis by blood, but aren't *we* related?" At this moment, Jal Uncle had discreetly taken the two *mobeds* aside and asked them to perform some unnecessary errands elsewhere to spare them the abuses that continued from the other side of the locked gate.

"If they won't allow me, at least let my mother be allowed to pay her respects to her *sahib*? She ate his *namak* but she also helped him to produce *me*, *seth*. Look, here I am, after all these years, your *sagaa* bastard-brother, and his other son. *Sala suars*. They called my mother, a—a—sorry sirs, I can't. I can't quite repeat that horrible word. *Sala suars*. Sala—"

Somehow, Jal Uncle succeeded in placating the young man who continued to protest even after his weeping mother tried to restrain him, but not before Kersi had reassured him. "Come tomorrow to my apartment and we shall talk things over." He remembered Trivikarma bursting into a piercingly high arc of laughter.

"Talk things over? Did you hear that, Ayee?" Trivikarma shouted to his mother in Marathi. Then reverting to English, he addressed Kersi. "Talking things over is not going to help, Kersi *seth*. We shall be coming to your apartment on June 21st, exactly at 3 p.m. That's three days from now. And when I say we are coming, Kersi *seth*, I mean for good! Do you follow?

"You have a big apartment on the 18th floor, don't you? We'll start our new life from there, okay, *seth*?

"I have always wanted to occupy one of them in Bombay's ultra-modern skyscrapers. That way I'll be able to improve on the models when *I* build them in the future. Why, don't you know? I am a full-fledged licensed architect. Your father invested a lot of money in my becoming one. Now I have to repay him. And where better to start than from where he had lived and from where my mother had slaved for him all her life. His *bali* is ready to leave, but my *bali* is about to begin. *Chal,* Ayee. Let's leave these respectable people to honour their dead amongst themselves. It gives us no *shoba* to be with them. Remember, *seth*. Three p.m. June 21st."

The shock of having an entire family, and that too an illegitimate one, being suddenly imposed on him, literally out of the blue, so to speak, made Kersi hate his dear departed father all the more in death than what he had when he was alive. It was as if he had been pushed out into another world that he had never seen or experienced in any of the thousand videos that he possessed. He was angry even at Jal Uncle when the latter whispered to him that he had known about Trivikarma for a long, long time.

They were now walking to the tower of silence clutching a piece of white cloth between them as Parsi mourners are supposed to during the *paidus.* They allowed the others to go forward while they retreated to a discreet distance in order to bring everything out into the open. "Why didn't Dad tell me about Janakibai being his… his…and Trivikarma being my...?" Kersi muttered fiercely.

"Would that have changed your life?" Jal Uncle responded wryly. "You live in your large room surrounded by your God knows 30 TVs and videos. You've spent your last 30 years only flipping channels. Is that an achievement? All that you have ever clutched in your life is a bloody remote control. Kersi, my boy, tell me, have you ever looked at the sky, for once, from your 18th floor window? Have you ever felt an actual road with your feet like the one we are walking on now? Have you ever allowed even our damn Bombay sun to shine on you? I am glad that your father's death has at least brought you outdoors for a change!"

"But they are coming to stay with me, Jal Uncle. Stop talking about roads and skies and the sun. Didn't you hear him? That's, that's absurd. Can't *you* get some kind of... some kind of *legal* order or whatever you call it to stop that from happening. I mean..." Kersi couldn't go on.

"I can, Kersi, but you know what, I won't. Behramsa wouldn't have liked that," replied Jal Uncle. Things were now really slipping out of control. Kersi was shocked.

"But he is dead, Jal Uncle. Look, there he is, mute on the *khandyaas*' shoulders. In a few minutes the vultures will make mince meat out of him. O God. I'm sorry. I'm truly truly sorry that I said that. I didn't mean to. Honest, Jal Uncle, I didn't. O God."

Jal Uncle quietly tugged at the white cloth they were holding. "Quiet. Now don't *you* make a scene as your brother did. Try and understand this. Trivikarma *was* his son too. Even though he could not present him as one to the world when he was alive, your father was secretly very proud of him. Maybe *you* can introduce him as *your* brother to the world from now on. After all, Janakibai *has* been like a mother to you, even if she was your father's, well, you know, what? They'll stay with you, but how you will treat them, well, that is entirely up to you. *You* decide! Maybe Trivikarma will help you. He *is* a very resourceful young man. You know, he never let your father's hopes down. Not even once. Look how hard he has studied to become an architect."

"About *you*, however, I'm sorry to say this, especially now, your father *never* had any hope. That is why he gave you your own remote control world. You don't have to prove anything in that world. Maybe you'll learn something valuable out of all this *tamasha*, Kersi *seth*. *Seth*, indeed! You are so used to your soap operas on your TV and video. Let's see how you cope in the one real life will shortly offer you."

Kensi yanked the white cloth so suddenly that it fell down on the dirty ground. Jal Uncle quickly picked it up and put it in his pocket. Then taking out a fresh white cloth he gave it to Kersi to hold. From the corner of his eyes he could see two vultures calmly flying towards the well in anticipation of their upcoming meal. He looked at his watch. It was nearing 3 p.m.

~

At 3 p.m. on June 21st, the doorbell to Kersi Palkhiwalla's 18th floor apartment promptly rang. An agitated Kersi opened the door to welcome his new family in.

"Poor people never keep rich people waiting, Kersi *seth*," said Trivikarma, calmly walking in, followed by his dazed mother, Janakibai. Since she was familiar with the large apartment she tended every day, she quickly took their meagre belongings and was making her way to the servants' *kohlis* when Trivikarma stopped her. "Where do you think you are going, *Ayee*? To the servants' *kohli*? But *we* haven't employed a servant yet, have we, Kersi *seth*? No. You will go into our father's bedroom. Yes. The same room where I was accidentally conceived. Now, which one is it? Which one?"

Janakibai burst into tears, and flinging her belongings to the floor, ran into the kitchen. Kersi tried to follow her but Trivikarma prevented him. "Let her cry, *seth*. Let her cry. All her life she has cried. Leave her alone. Women like her are taught to be dumb, first by our *shastras* and our *karmas*, and then by rich people like you and your father. So they suffer their entire lives and when they die, they die dumb. So let her cry. It is what *Parmeshwara* wants. Damn *Parmeshwara*. He will no more make her destiny, Kersi *seth*. Nor will he make mine. I'll see to that. I'll see to that. *I'll* make her destiny and I'll make my own destiny. Ah, and I'll most certainly change *yours* as well. Says Trivikarma: It's all a question of height."

Kersi listened and watched, dumbfounded. How tall Trivikarma suddenly seemed to grow as he slowly took possession of all the space all around him. His scornful words seemed to literally add extra feet and inches to him. Jal Uncle had called him "resourceful," but he was really much more than that. Kersi couldn't find words to describe this...this...so-called brother of his.

Trivikarma, now immensely taller and stronger, was standing on the balcony. Kersi had shrunk back against the wall. His fingers itched for the remote controls which were lying all over his bed. He wanted to run into his room, grab hold of them, and switch on all 30 video sets just to erase this scene and silence that loud, mocking, arrogant voice.

When Trivikarma spoke again, he seemed to have grown almost as tall as the ceiling. "It is, as I said, Kersi *seth*, all a question of height. Do you know why your father purchased this flat on the 18th floor? It wasn't just for the scenery, you know. Height to him meant success. He worked at an office which was on the 15th floor; so, he had to live much above it where his success would be visible not only to himself but also to others. Only a man with a strong determination makes it to the top these days, *seth*. *I* was always at the top of my class too. Yes, me. Look at me, the one they always called the *gangabaicha moolga*. At first that hurt. But later it became a matter of pride to me. There I was, *seth*, a *gangabaicha moolga*, but always at the top of my class. But the only problem was that I lived in a slum. Think about it, *seth*.

"Slums don't grow tall overnight. They merely spread out horizontally every day. Now, you cannot make your success visible horizontally. Slums, *seth*, are like epidemics. They spread like a fever. And once you become a part of a slum, you are *seen* as a slum too. There is no hope and no respect for horizontal people like us, *seth*. But for the vertical ones like you and your father and all these good residents of Bali Apartments, no one questions you or them when, like your father, you secretly visit us slum dwellers for your private pleasures and entertainment. You are not supposed to fall in our eyes. So, after visiting us, you come back like your father to your 18th-floor apartment and you go back, the next day, to your 15th-floor office.

"These are high and mighty structures, but they rise, Kersi *seth*, from all the shit, and the dirt and the rubble that are constantly spat and shat upon to make all of us who are already a part of it, look so small and so insignificant. Always. Come here and look below. LOOK BELOW, *SETH*."

Kersi went obediently to the balcony and looked down. Then pulling himself up as high as he could get, he spat out: "But wasn't my father good to you and your mother? He even advised Jal Uncle, I mean Jal *seth*, not to bring any legal action against you. He, he, even paid for your education. He made you into, into an…an…an architect, didn't he? Didn't he?"

Trivikarma howled with laughter and grew a full 10 feet taller. "*Arrey, seth*. You think, the great Behramsa, our father, did all this for us? Forget all those painted women in your TVs and videos and look for a moment, just for a moment, at my mother. Yes, *my* mother, that poor, silent, dumb Jankibai who right now is weeping in the kitchen. Yes. That same Janakibai, in whom our father found the woman he had never had or loved in his life. Whether he took her on our dirty slum floor or in any of these carpeted rooms, it was always for *his* pleasure, you hear, *his* pleasure. So it was natural that in me, *Kersi seth*, he also found the son he could never have in you. Don't you see? He wanted someone to continue *his* high name, *his* towering success, after he was gone. That is why *I* am here. He made *me* an architect to perpetuate *his* success.

"Ah, *Ayee*. Come. Show me the room where I was conceived. SHOW ME! I want to begin building my dreams from there. Then they won't smell of the slums. And you can come too, Kersi *seth*. Let us celebrate this moment as one big, happy family.

"O, your father told us a lot about you. But don't worry, I have arrived now. So has mother. We'll give *you* a whole new perspective on life. You'll learn all about heights and depths from me. I'll make you measure them every single day. I promise. You know, *seth*. Architecture gives you a whole new meaning about living and dying that your TVs and videos can't. It does, *seth*. It really does."

Trivikarma kept on growing for Kersi as he talked. At times he looked and sounded so much like his father. The moment he commanded, he was obeyed. So Kersi mutely followed the tearful Janakibai as she led them both to his father's spacious bedroom.

"There it is, *seth*, there it is. Look at that four-poster bed on which our father *fucked* my mother. Poor woman. She won't understand *that* profane English word! But then, she has lived with so much profanity, *Seth*, that it would not shock her even if I told her *what* it meant! This will be my room now. We'll give the neighbouring one to her. You already have yours. *Nakoo*, *nakoo*, *Ayee*, you will not sit on *that* bed," and then quickly switching to Marathi, he cautioned his mother against even touching that bed. It was, he told her, strictly "out of bounds" for her. Then taking her gently, he led her to the next room which had belonged to Kersi's mother and told her it was hers from now onwards.

Coming back, Trivikarma firmly took Kersi by the shoulders and propelled him towards Behramsa's four-poster bed. "Now, you, *seth*, are welcome to sit on it," he began, but Kersi cut him off. "Why do you keep calling me, *seth*. I...I don't like that."

Trivikarma once again burst into laughter. "What does it matter what *you* like or don't like, *seth*," he mocked spreading himself out horizontally on the large bed. He seemed to fit its entire length completely. "Do you want to know why I shall keep calling you *seth*, *seth*? Come here and sit down at the foot of the bed. Not so far. Come closer. Good. Now, while I stretch all over the bed, you *seth*, will stretch out on the floor. That's right. No. No. Your head on the floor should be roughly below my feet on the bed. Yes, in the *opposite* direction. There. That's perfect. Now, you see *Seth*, when my father was busy fucking mother, she was up here on the bed with him. But after he had finished, she was told to get down on the floor and sleep exactly in the same position that you are sleeping in now. And she always obeyed. Why? The answer is very simple. He was the *seth*. So remember *that* when every time I call *you seth*. It's all, says Trivikarma, a question of height."

Kersi couldn't stand it anymore. He got up from the floor, rushed to his room, and locked it. He collected all the clickers and put on one by one, all 30 TVs and videos. He didn't care what channels he was furiously flicking through. He sat on the middle of his untidy bed and felt a curious sensation of shrinking. He turned up the volumes of all his machines to drown the peals of Trivikarma's laughter emanating from his father's room. He started clicking furiously. The sound of the Parsi priests performing the *gatha*s assaulted him from one channel. How had they managed to crawl into the Discovery Channel? Was he imagining this? He switched to another. Someone called Professor Fiske, dressed as a *mobed*, was talking about the "Sears Tower of Silence." He switched to another. A Hindu lawyer, in front of an entire anglophile *adalat*, was calling the accused man who had slain his Parsi architect partner, "resourceful."

Throwing the clickers on the bed, Kersi rushed towards the huge window which he had always kept closed. Wrenching it open, he was surprised to see a sky of pristine blue. There was not a single cloud in it. A bright sun was shining. As he turned to one of his TV screens, he screamed. There, in close-up, was the hideous image of a vulture slowly masticating something in its enormously powerful jaws. Strands of *kasti* seemed to be wrapped all around its bloody beak.

MOUTHWASH

Why wasn't the queue moving fast enough? Vinda's left palm had got all wet clutching the "exact change" in his pocket. These days, everyone in Bombay wanted "exact change" except waiters, barbers, *hamaals* and cab-drivers. They went a step further and refused to give you any "change" that was due.

The man ahead of him grumbled that it was no fun seeing a "two-hour film if they expect you to wait for a ticket for two-and-a-half hours! This city is slowly but surely going to the dogs. Don't you agree?" Vinda did not reply, but instinctively turned his face away. He waited for the regular taunt about him "being rude" or "being too educated" to answer to follow. But it did not come. Piqued by Vinda's silent-face rebuff, the speaker instead found himself face-to-face with the old Parsi ticket seller.

"If you can stand in the ration line for half a day to get your *daal* and your *chawal*, why do you grumble about standing in line for a film?"

"Because this is supposed to entertain me, *bawaji*, not feed my stomach."

"All right, smart aleck. Next time come on roller skates and entertain those who are standing behind you before your turn comes. Next?"

A harassed, wizened face slowly appeared to take shape behind the glass ticket booth's cut-out circle. Instinctively,Vinda turned his face away and took out a piece of paper on which he had written "Three tickets please. And here's the exact change", and thrust it at the ticket seller.

"What's wrong with you, *mishtur*? You're a high-caste Brahmin or something or do you suffer from..."

"BAD BREATH?" Vinda's angry retort surprised everyone standing in line. Taking out a pencil, he wrote in large, bold capitals—"THREE TICKETS PLEASE AND KINDLY SHUT YOUR MOUTH!" As he raised his pencil to jab the dot under that last exclamation, the lead point broke.

The man behind the glass giggled loudly. Slowly he took out a small silver snuff-box. Taking a pinch of snuff between his fingers, he applied it hideously across his filthy brown front teeth. Then, tearing three tickets with those same dirty, snuff-smeared fingers, he leaned his face deliberately towards the cutout glass circle and spat out in a foul, snuff-infested breath, "Here, *fonny* man. Take them with my compliments and enjoy..."

Vinda grabbed the tickets and rushed towards the theatre's entrance. Thrusting all three of them into the palms of the astonished usher, he rushed to the toilet. Locking the door firmly behind him, he slammed down the commode lid, and sat on it. Raising one of his palms, he breathed suspiciously into it.

Did his breath really stink? Or was he just imagining that it did? Then why is it that nobody had even been friendly with him in school, not even the tall boys who usually liked bullying the short ones? *He* was short, but for some strange reason they had always left *him* alone. They never even came close to him. And then, why had he never, even once, had his test papers actually handed to him by his teachers as they did with the other students? They were always thrown at him from a distance, as though, as though... And yet, his family had never seemed to mind.

His father, who had always been distant from him, had tragically drowned in a polluted and stinking river when he went to take his bath on his last pilgrimage to Benares. His mother, who bathed three times a day, especially after working the entire morning with the low-caste servant, was now bed-ridden and literally stank from her sick bed. As for his sister? Her exhausted existence constantly left her smelling as she shuttled daily between her stale telexes; her tired shorthand pads and a foul-mouthed bullying boss who perspired terribly in his small air-conditioned office. To top it all, there was the threatening smelly landlord who always scratched his balls every time he came around asking for the delayed rent payment. All his life had been spent in tiny rooms that daily bore the antiseptic smells of Dettol and urine, phenyl and shit. "Stink" had been so inherent to his family. Maybe, *that* was why they could not smell *his* bad breath's daily contribution to it.

He sat on the commode for a long time. He would sit here till the intermission. He was only interested in the main feature and didn't mind going in a little late. He wouldn't have to worry about his immediate neighbours in the dark since there would be none sitting on either side of him. That is why he always bought three tickets whenever he went by himself to see any film. Then his bad breath could comfortably "respire and expire". That was how *he* had summed up the nature of his alienation to Old Padamsee, who lived just above him. Yes. It would "respire and expire" in that anonymous dark of the cinema which he frequented as it provided him with such a comfortable and convenient refuge in this heartless and breathless city.

It was nearing interval time and the bathroom would soon get crowded. The rituals of the mouth had to be hurriedly completed. He took out a small compact case from his pocket. His tailor had always wondered why he insisted on having such huge pockets. Anaita had given him this compact case last Christmas.

One by one, he took out the various nose and mouth "drops" and started putting them alternately, first in his mouth and then in each nostril. Next, he took out a special packet of herbal powder he had got from a convincing quack sitting outside Andheri Station and proceeded to apply it liberally across his teeth with his fingers. But it became brown and stained them like that old fellow's snuff. He suddenly looked so *"fonny"* standing there, his second finger poised before his teeth. Disgusted, he washed it out, and threw the packet away.

He looked at all these tiny bottles sleeping innocently on top of each other in his case. Every month, half his salary went in purchasing them. He bought everything that science, TV and radio commercials, a passing remark overheard in a bus or train, or the merchandise that peddlers, touts and shady Chinese dentists operating in narrow, dirty rooms had to offer.

He had shrugged off even a promising banking career and had joyously taken the freely available position of the timid, "faceless," and remotely desk-d municipal clerk.

That unfortunate adjective had been imposed on him by Old Padamsee: "You didn't want to work in the bank," he had roared at Vinda one day, "because you thought your so-called imaginary bad breath would scare people away from investing in your bank, didn't you? O, you damn fool. Instead of sitting in an air-conditioned bank counter, counting cash, making entries in the ledger and chatting closely with your customers, you now sit in that stinking hole of a municipal building, amongst tons and tons of ant-eaten files, writing ridiculous reports in triplicates. And you like the job, don't you? Oh yes, you do. Don't deny it. And do you know why? Let me tell you. Municipal clerks don't have faces. They are not expected to. That is what you wanted, didn't you? Because then, nobody could come close to you, or stand over your desk, or even lean closer when instructing you.

"Now some do, but you don't mind *them*, because these peasants are your *mooniceepul* colleagues, with little bundles of *tambaku* tucked away in the corners of their mouths. And their *tambaku* stinks as much as you think your damned imaginary foul breath does, doesn't it?"

There had been a lot of truth in what Old Padamsee had said, and yet the old man himself was connected to the 'idea' of stink. In fact, they had met because of what they later affectionately referred to as the "Father Zosima" incident.

Vinda had often passed Old Padamsee on the stairs but had never paid much attention to him. He was a nondescript old man who was vaguely known by his tenants through certain reported facts like how he had his *bun-maska* at Café Williams around the corner twice a day: once in the morning before he caught bus no. 48 to work, and once after returning from work.

He remembered the day when they had first met. It had promised to be the usual Bombay Sunday of well-dressed churchgoers and folded-hand prayers in the morning at the churches; enthusiastic gabardine-worn and sari-clad race-course betters in the afternoon at the race-course, and energetic families descending towards Chowpatty for spicy *bhel*, refreshing coconut water, and cold *kulfi* in the evening.

But before that Sunday could actually stretch out and yawn away all the fatigues of the previous week, a noisy commotion had suddenly erupted on the staircase. Vinda had come out with a towel in his hand. It seemed as if someone had actually fallen down the stairs. There was another crash followed by Mrs. Padamsee's harsh strident voice. "Take away these filthy books and clean them out for once, you hear. Or if you don't want to do that, just throw them away. I won't have them polluting my room and my flowers."

And down they had come: fat, dirty, pencil-marked, dog-eared volumes of the collected works of Balzac, Chekhov, Conrad, Dostoyevsky, Dickens. "If you revere them so much, then why don't you clean them up once in a while? As it is you buy them cheap and dirty from those footpath vendors. It's like picking up flowers that somebody has thrown on the dirty road."

And then Old Padamsee had come down, shouting at the top of *his* voice. "I revere what's *in* them, you ignorant woman. And what's *in* them can never stink, you hear. I don't *have* to *clean* them or *wipe* the pages like the water you keep changing in your damn flower vases. *That* stinks. *That* pollutes. *These* and *these* and *these* DON'T."

Vinda had watched the old man as he painstakingly picked up the volumes, fondling and cradling them in his arms as though they had broken a hand or a leg or had hurt themselves in their rude and furious tumble down the stairs.

Vinda had run forward to help Old Padamsee. He had always imagined this cantankerous old man as probably someone who had retired on a small pension, but was still working as an usher in a seedy suburban cinema hall, or oiling one of those big clumsy wheels in some ancient Iranian's wheezing ice-factory, or checking coats, briefcases and umbrellas in old philanthropic Parsi libraries like J.B. Petit's at Flora Fountain. But now he thought differently. Giving such dignity to these books gave dignity to the one who was holding them like a proud father in his arms.

Later that evening, Old Padamsee had invited Vinda for tea. "Why does that silly wife of mine make such a fuss over stink? But how could she know? She's only an ignorant flower decorator. People who design beauty often are, you know. She decorates wedding-stages so that afterwards children can run amuck and tear all the flowers to shreds. She designs flower-baskets for patients in intensive care-units so that they can be placed conveniently to actually hide the problematic monitored heartbeats from the patient as they weakly flicker away on borrowed electricity on those hospital screens. If the water stinks, she changes the water. But if the flowers stink, she merely throws them away for they have outlived their purpose. Silly woman. Talks to *me* about polluting the room. Forgive me, my son. I'm an old man. I like to rant about these little things. But you. Tell me, what do you think?"

And Vinda's foul mouth, suffused with the remnants of all kinds of powders, drops, taunts and sinuses had suddenly broken forth in a fierce flood of communication. It seemed as though someone had finally changed the waters of his breaths in that stinking vase—his cursed mouth. He talked and talked and talked till he finally felt he had finally exhausted the very source of its stink. Suddenly he shut up, and in that silence, he imagined how Mrs. Padamsee changed all the stinking water in all her vases and threw away all the old dead flowers. Then he spoke, "If my mother stinks, especially those who have come to meet her, the world at least, pities her for it. But when I—"

"And your world doesn't, so you feel resentful," replied Old Padamsee. "But how can it when you don't push your face towards it. You are constantly *turning* your face away from it. Why don't you amuse the world, or at least scare it with your so-called foul breath once in a while? Have you ever tried that? Let it make its own judgment. And since you are so concerned about stink, let me show you something." He removed from the tossed-up pile of books a battered copy of Dostoyevsky's *The Brothers Karamazov*. He picked out a certain passage and asked Vinda to read it quietly to himself.

Vinda had read it slowly. It described the dead body of a holy man, one Father Zosima, who was placed in the centre of the room. As the mourners filed past it, they suddenly became aware of an awful stink emanating from the corpse. One by one they quickly left the room, confounding and confusing the pious Alyosha about his dead master's consistent claims to sanctity and purity when he had been alive.

Vinda had looked up at Old Padamsee and the old man had put a finger on his lips. He remembered noticing how clean the old man's fingers had been in spite of all the dirt on the books. "You have lived too long with yourself, my son. That was Alyosha's problem too. Now that we have met over Father Zosima's stinking dead body, let me introduce you to a young lady, Anaita Xaviers. This is her address. Go to her, especially when you feel alone and lonely. Tell her I sent you. Like you, she is all alone too. She will help you much more than I can. And remember," and here Old Padamsee had paused, "her water needs changing too. Like yours. Like mine. Like all of ours."

Vinda put away the bottles into the compact case. He emerged from the bathroom calmer than what he had been when he had rushed in. After the next two hours, spent comfortably in that darkness that now awaited him, he decided he would go to Anaita's.

~

He watched Anaita making the bed and smoothing the sheet and pillows. She treated her bed with the same kind of sanctity with which Old Padamsee treated his books. She always made the bed after they had finished making love. Did she do that with all the others too? Maybe she did it deliberately in his presence to remove all traces of both clumsiness and expertise that the act of successful lovemaking always demanded.

To make him feel comfortable and at home, on the first day, he had visited her, Vinda remembered, how she had talked about her own "fall from grace". That was how she had defined it. And that confessional recitation had invoked from him, almost spontaneously, his own lapses that he termed as his "bad breath moments".

"I was seduced a long time ago, Vinda, by a frightened young man who was, you won't believe me, actually preparing for priesthood. I really don't know what happened to him. Some say he ran away. Some say he killed himself. Anyway, in order to wipe out *our* disgrace, I mean, my family's disgrace, my elder sister, was forced to take the veil after I adamantly refused. Someone had to endorse our Xavier family name. Poor thing. She was chosen. And she did not resist."

"You know Indian families and how *they* insist on sacrifices. Now, prayers and penitence are fine. They feed the soul very well, but the stomach has to be fed each day and the rent has to be paid each month, and *this* is the only way I can do both because I've never had any miraculous Xavier in the family to depend upon. One by one they all left me till I was completely alone. Some are still living in this city. Others have become quick victims to kitchen-brewed hooch. It's fairly regular in our community. One sister was left with perpetual black clothes and handcuffed rosaries. As for me, as you can see, a conspicuous lack of clothes is what my survival really depends on once I abrogate my daily hours of decency."

She worked at this adjunct profession, only in the evenings. She refused to tell Vinda what she did during the rest of her day. It was Old Padamsee who solved that mystery for him. "O, she works with me at a suburban Social Services Mandal. Suburban, my dear Vinda, suburban, because that is where all the slums of our city are. You won't find our city's pure and *swadeshi* white sari clad Lakshmis and white *kurta*-d Lakshmans dirtying their hands and feet there. Or contributing their decently earned cash, either. O, no! Only polluted people know what stink really is and how it can be served."

How accurately had the old man summed it all up. And every time when he went to her, as he was doing right now in the cab, it was literally to clean himself and get rid of all the stink that, in addition to his bad breath, the world had piled on him during the course of that day. And he had been so grateful because she had been the second person to actually tackle his stink, literally confront it after Old Padamsee had managed to first dislodge its heavy lid that day in his room. True, salvation had not yet come, but at least a beginning had been made.

He still remembered Anaita's definition of stink when he had first explained his bad breath obsession to her. "Bad breath, my deluded lover boy, is really no different from our menstruation. It's actually good for one from time to time. It cleans the womb by expelling all that is not wanted from it. So let your bad breath come out. But, don't let it spread into every part of you as you've let yours. I suffer from my periods too. That is why I never allow anyone to make love to me during my periods. Why shouldn't I be intimate with my own womb, especially when it stinks. And you know something, I actually like that smell. No. No. I really do. What matters is not 'foul' breath or 'sweet' breath, but breath itself. Why make such a fuss about it that it ruins your life? Breath is breath. Sometimes it is sweet and sometimes it is sour. And like periods, it requires no further adjectives. Why do you insist on giving it so many?"

In two days it would be Christmas. The cab was moving slowly. Traffic was heavy on the roads. Vinda looked out of the cab's window. People were busy doing a lot of last-minute Christmas shopping. The Christmas spirit was in the air but still that "smell" of Christmas was somehow missing. It was no use taking Anaita out in the crowded and noisy city on Christmas. He would borrow Old Padamsee's car and take her for a quiet, long drive, maybe down the Navynagar area of town. It was always so quiet and peaceful there. Besides, it was so close to the sea. There would be no disturbances there except, perhaps, the distant noises of drunken sailors celebrating far away in their isolated naval barracks. And if, by chance, a drunken sailor suddenly emerged and tried to disturb them, he would frighten him away by breathing his foul air all over his face like the proverbial dragon.

Vinda smiled to himself like a man conscious of a terrible secretive power he could unleash every time the world crept very close to him.

Old Padamsee had agreed instantly to give his car, but he had not liked the idea of his two young friends going to such a lonely spot, especially on Christmas. Why couldn't they enjoy being alone with themselves within a crowd? However, this was not the day to preach to them. So when the day arrived, he gave him the car keys, and deliberately brought his old face very close to Vinda's. Holding it tightly in his palm, so that the other's habitual instinct would not turn it away, Old Padamsee said, "A Very Happy Christmas to you, my son, and also to you, my daughter. You are like my very own children. Now keep your faces together and drive very carefully. That's a very lonely area, you know. So be careful." Vinda smiled and wished the old man too. He started the car and turned to wave at him. Old Padamsee waved back and Vinda saw the glint of sudden tears in the old man's eyes as they turned the corner.

Anaita didn't say much that evening. There were tears in her eyes too. "It's nothing, Vinda. I've just got my period and don't feel so good. Besides, everything's so quiet and peaceful here. Words seem so totally out of place." And they did. So, he stopped the car and they got out. A few feet away lay the ocean. In a few hours it would be Christmas. The tide had started coming in slowly.

Watching the folds of water settling so regularly and calmly on the shore, Vinda had the sudden urge to go and wash his face in that water. Maybe even gargle in it. Maybe the "salt" of the ocean would freshen his foul breath a little. So, he left Anaita and started walking towards the ocean's generously available liquid. He had hardly taken a few steps when he heard a sharp intake of her breath followed by a muffled scream.

Vinda turned around and ran towards Anaita. Two white forms had suddenly materialised behind her and she was struggling. Blindly, Vinda lashed out at one and smelt the mixed odour of alcohol and vomit and blood.

He lashed out again and something heavy fell backwards in the darkness. He tore Anaita loose and pushed her away. The other form was now instantly on him, and soon Vinda felt himself being slowly crushed. A hideous face suddenly loomed all over him literally stinking of stale liquor. Let it come nearer, Vinda thought. Let it come nearer. It can't match my breath. It can't. Nothing can. Nothing can. That's why those tall boys couldn't bully me in school.

"Respire! Expire! Respire! Expire!" Those words were now screaming inside his mind as though he was literally sucking them out from the mouth of a drowned victim. The face was coming closer. Mrs. Padamsee was changing the water in her vases. The face was now almost on top of his, and he could hear the tide. The tide was coming in. COMING IN. Then Vinda opened his mouth and LET OUT an eternity of stink.

"Vinda! Vinda!" That was Anaita's voice. Why was she shouting? Didn't she have confiden...

The knife had go...ne in... How easily it came out and went in again... He could distinctly hear the roar of the tide. Suddenly, there was no face over his. No weight. He felt light. Had he scared that face? HAD HE? But where was Anaita? Would she cry, later? Would his sister cry too? Would they tell his mother that her son, too, like her husband, had-had-what? Expired? And why was Old Padamsee wiping the tears and removing the dust from his fingernails, both at the same time?

"You damn fool. O, you damned fool. Why did you do it? O my darling. Why? Why?" Anaita was now kneeling all over him.

"I was try-ing to-to frigh-ten him..aw-ay..." The words painfully broke from his torn mouth slowly like bloody bubbles of mouthwash. With-with-my..ba-ad-bre-ath... but...I...I...couldn'-t. I...I..."

And he tried to laugh at his own absurdity. But before the laugh took away his life, she suddenly covered his mouth with hers. He struggled beneath her to move his face away, but she would not allow it. She had never kissed him on the lips before. Now she was going to. She wanted him to die with her mouth firmly planted on his lips.

Somebody switched on the headlights of the car and started playing with the engine. He had stopped breathing under her for some time, but she didn't remove her lips from his. Somebody was racing the engine now and deliberately speeding it up. But she still lay there as if she too was dead over him. Somebody switched off the headlights, then switched them on again. She still did not move. She would wait like that till Christmas, pretending to be dead before the wise men from the city finally arrived.

144 TUGHLAQ KUTIR

"But why do you want to go to America?" Dada asked, his knife and fork poised over the rapidly shrinking egg on his plate. I noticed his fingernails. They were pink and carefully clipped round the edges.

"So that when a girl takes out a cigarette and lights it in public at a restaurant table, she doesn't have all the patrons, including the figures in the paintings on the wall, turn around and look at her. And that's only *one* of the reasons."

I watched my mocking words settle amongst the quiet occupants at the breakfast table. Dada lowered his eyes and now gave his full attention to the egg. He separated the white neatly from the yolk and proceeded to eat it without touching the yolk. Once the white had disappeared, he balanced the yolk perfectly on the fork and raised it carefully to his mouth and swallowed it whole so that it did not stain his wonderful white beard and moustache.

Bhabhi, his wife sitting opposite him, did not say anything. Her four tight white curls on the top of her head made her look almost like an aged schoolgirl who had stepped out of one of those illustrated comic books

I had read as a child. She kept piling most of the bread slices in her plate, and then proceeded to separate the hard crusts from the soft centres. Soon, a large pile of hard crusts started to collect in the centre of her plate.

Arjun, their son (and Uncle Arjun to me), sat quietly hunched up in his chair. The eyes behind his thick glasses were glued to the cold glass of milk before him. With his thumb he was idly wiping away the misty frost that formed on the outside of the glass. As he would wipe a broad vertical stroke, the glass's surface would become clear for a moment and then slowly start to frost all over again. As he started on his next vertical stroke, it made *me* suddenly realise, that as a guest who had arrived to pay them a weekend visit, while on a trip with friends to Delhi, I would have to do most of the talking.

"My dear Premi," Dada said, finally wiping his plate clean with a last piece of bread firmly anchored to his fork, "if you had only met my daughter Lajwanti before she...died. You both would have got along very well. When Mahatma Gandhi—and don't *you* ever refer to him merely as Gandhi, young lady, please, not in this house. Well, as I was saying, when Mahatma Gandhi gave the call to the Indian nation to stop using British goods and clothing as part of our nationalistic protest, you know what she did? With one sweep of her hand, mind you, with just one sweep of her hand, she scattered," and he paused, for he was an old hand at oratory, "the entire British Empire on the floor. Yes, my darling girl, there it lay among countless broken perfume bottles, lipsticks, compact cases, and yes, she proceeded to scatter all her clothes too—the likes of which you will never see today. Pleated skirts, tweeds, exquisitely tailored puffed up blouses, and what not. She even started to empty her bookshelves but fortunately I prevented her from doing that. Knowledge should not be so readily discarded." Sometimes it seemed as though he was talking entirely to himself, which as I came to learn, was quite a common trait with Dada. "Of course, we did consign a few Imperialist English authors to the floor like that ass Macaulay and all those dreadful dreadful 'History of India' books written by enlightened, but misguided Englishmen, of course, like Father Gense and Henry Rawlinson. But certainly not our Rudyard Kipling. Not *that* man with his mongooses, his half-breeds, his Kims and his Gunga Dins."

I laughed along with him, then abruptly stopped. Uncle Arjun and his mother remained silent. Between the two of them, they had not even produced a blush.

Bhabhi got up and dutifully started pouring the tea. I looked at Dada's serene face, so pink that bright morning. What struck me most was the intonation with which he spoke his words. It made his imposing physical appearance all the more impeccable. It was such a delight to hear good Queen's English spoken the first thing in the morning, especially on an Indian breakfast table. And such a paradox too! Here I was listening to one of India's great freedom-fighters condemning the very race from whom he had imbibed, not only a mastery over an alien tongue, but such exquisite table manners to go with it as he had demonstrated a short while back, in the eating of that fried egg. Not once had that yolk been punctured. And all this, from a man who all his life had borne that *other* yolk—his country's—so cheerfully and so defiantly.

"I sometimes wish the British had not left India, Dada," I replied. "What a mess we seem to have made of our own country. I know this would seem to be yet another cliché expressed so rampantly and rashly, but let's face it. The only pride we have and which we so openly flaunt to everyone doesn't really belong to us but to our ancestors. Look at the city of Delhi itself. I feel like a foreign tourist marvelling at its edifices. And its architectural grandeur really belongs to the *firangis,* not us. Our government functions in buildings like Rashtrapati Bhavan. But weren't they built by the British? We invite people from all over the world to come see our Taj Majal and our Fatehpur Sikri, both built by the Mughals. We take our families for picnics in the Lodhi Gardens and tell our children tall tales about the Qutub Minar. But who were the Lodhis? Who were the Qutub-ud-dins? Not Indians, but invaders who settled here. As for..."

"And do you also know the names of all those foreign administrators, Premi," Dada quietly interrupted me, "who took a pencil, one day, and drew a carefully measured and calculated line right across our land's face to divide it into two separate nations? Of course, they did it on a brightly coloured map in a large, fairly well-lit room and, I'm sure, under all the benign eyes of their so-called framed monarchs. But can you imagine, my educated young lady, can you imagine a house, an ordinary Indian house, being divided in that way? Can you visualise a family being amputated, a culture being recklessly overturned by just, just one stroke of a pencil? That was done by one of our ancestors too." He carefully removed the film of cream that had appeared on the surface of his tea. "Think about it. If your baby happened to be sleeping in a cot, and if you happened to be cooking in the kitchen, and if that pencil's line ran through the middle of your house, do you know what would have happened when the soldiers came? Your baby would have been taken away, perhaps on a mule's back, perhaps in a crowded train to a new place in a new country that would be named, hereafter, Pakistan, or Hindustan, while you, dear girl, if you were not raped, God forbid, you would be running, yes, running empty-handed and empty-bellied and to what? To the confused waters of a distant river called the Ganga or the Padma or to the equally agitated waters of some abandoned mosque's courtyard?"

I was effectively silenced, both by an authentic historian and by his convincing history. I felt a peculiar kind of shame crawling all over me like *dhobi*'s itch. Now I knew why Dada had not been so well-respected in our family. After all, what were we Sindhis compared to him but the usual market-rending merchants? Sure, we had prospered and done well for ourselves in a post-Independent India that we had chosen. Diamonds, perfumes, terelene shirts, we had a finger in all of those pies. Now we had ventured on a new occupation: financing our children's trips to America. For "further studies", we proudly proclaimed when everybody enquired. And here was Dada, that other kind of Sindhi who had said a simple goodbye to all his relatives on an Indian station platform a long, long time ago. Like many of us, he had made that painful trip instigated by that pencil. Like many of us, he had chosen India as his homeland. But unlike many of us, he had picked up his small bundle of belongings, handed over his railway tickets at the gate, and with his wife and two small children, he had literally walked from that Indian station straight into the Freedom Movement, which in those days, erupted all over every street and every lane of India. He had been jailed innumerable times. He had lost his only daughter, first to a sudden mental illness, and then, to a harsh inevitable death. But even that had not broken his spirit. Even after the British had left, he still insisted on serving the ruling Indian Ministry, if not directly, then at least in a purely advisory capacity. Our myopic Indian government, of course, hardly consulted him on any issues these days. But out of respect for all that he had sacrificed during the Independence struggle, the government gave him a miserly monthly pension and this rambling mansion, 144 Tughlaq Kutir, "for services rendered in the past", as they so bureaucratically put it in the coloniser's language.

This house was his life, although the people he shared it with, strangely appeared lifeless. His wife, who everyone called Bhabhi, was an illiterate girl whom he had married according to his father's dying wishes. His son Arjun was presently jobless though once he had ventured to make a couple of film documentaries on India for the Film's Division.

All this information I had gleaned from my family in the occasional references that were made to "Dada" and his strange *parivar*, especially on important festival days, when everybody who was anybody in the family got together. And here he was, actually sitting across me at the table, wiping his mouth carefully with a napkin. "Well, young lady, no more sermons over breakfast plates.

We shall meet in the evening. I have some work to attend to now and it's been a long, long time since I've talked with one of my own."

His eyes dimmed for a moment. He couldn't get himself to finish the sentence. We rose from the table, all except Uncle Arjun, who still remained hunched before his glass of milk. Neither he nor Bhabhi had said a single word, but I had noticed the look of pride on their faces when Dada had been speaking. It was a look that made me feel that these three people were somehow bound together inextricably, and nothing in the world would be able to sever that kind of an umbilical cord.

I picked up the dishes and followed Bhabhi to the kitchen. I could feel the chipped edges of the plates against my fingers as I carried them. Lowering them into the sink, I watched her as she soaped the vessels. Conversation with her was difficult. But I gave it a try. I commented how dreadful it was the way prices were going up. She repeated after me, "Yes." "Dreadful." "Very."

The kitchen was bare. A handful of spoons and forks, an odd assortment of bowls, two saucepans and some cups and saucers lay huddled in the drawers. Some of the handles of the drawers were dangling, but no one had bothered to fix them. On one of the shelves sat two large glass jars containing some dull-coloured spices. Going towards a basket suspended from the ceiling by a frayed wire, Bhabhi took out, what seemed to me, an ancient cauliflower and some thoroughly misshapen potatoes and started the laborious process of cutting them into tiny pieces.

Through the window in the kitchen I watched Uncle Arjun as he worked steadily in a small vegetable patch in the backyard. He went down slowly on his knees peering at the horizontal lanes of tomatoes through his thick spectacles. Prodding the earth with his fingers he examined the unripened tomatoes carefully, feeling their surfaces with his thumb, again and again, as he had done this morning on the cold surface of his glass of milk. Inside the kitchen, however, another cauliflower and some more shapeless potatoes fell as helpless sliced victims to Bhabhi's skilful knife strokes. Neatly arranging the peeled-off portions on the side of the sink, she swooped up the vegetable pieces, hurriedly washed them under the tap, and dumped them in the saucepan where the oil and spices were boiling.

I continued wiping the dishes. The roar of the frying vegetables and the sizzling of the spices seemed to save me from making any more unnecessary remarks.

I was about to leave the kitchen when Bhabhi placed her hand on my shoulder and quietly said, "Come." Taking out a chain of keys tied across her waist by a thin silver belt, she shuffled to a small closet-like drawer in the small passageway leading from the kitchen to the hall. Her huge wooden slippers made a harsh sound as they clanked all over the wooden floor. They seemed to speak much more than she did.

As the closet-door swung open, I noticed a small rectangular box from which she took out two pieces of English chocolates and shyly thrust them at me. Then, counting the remaining chocolates in the box, she suddenly whipped out a pencil and made a note of them on a piece of paper glued inside the box, and closed the lid. Shuffling back to the kitchen, she stirred the frugal meal of cauliflower and potatoes boiling over the ancient Primus stove. Its sides were caked with a horrible black layer of kerosene that generations had somehow neglected to wipe away.

I went up and quietly dried the last dish. Not to hurt the old woman, I deliberately made a big show about eating the chocolates before her. She looked up quietly, then concentrated on her cooking. I put the towels away and stepped out into the vegetable-garden patch.

There was no one in the garden so I decided to explore the house and the huge courtyard surrounding it. It was a rambling mansion, the likes of which I had never seen before. Moss seemed to have grown all over the outer walls. I turned the corner and stopped. A tennis-net sagged on an abandoned tennis court. It was almost hypnotic to watch that pronounced sag. I tried to turn the lever and tighten it up. But broken metal shreds crumbled into my palms. The iron, however, remained like tetanus, unyielding and hard. I gave up and walked on till I was under the front door. Over it, an arch of plaster hung like a hurriedly plucked-out eyebrow.

I was relieved when, turning the corner, I saw two little children of the servants playing in the outhouse. Although I had seen no servants in the house, Dada may have had a few to assist him in the house when he needed them.

The servant's outhouse was small and neatly kept. An old woman sat in the small portico picking out stones from the generous quantity of rice she had spread on the silver *thali*. She smiled at me as I passed by. I should have kept Bhabhi's English chocolates and given it to these two kids, a boy and a girl, who had shyly hidden themselves behind their old granny.

Inside the small house, a young woman was squatting beside her earthen-stove making fresh *chapatis*. Beside her stood a huge iron jar in which she had been pounding a heady mixture of chilly and spices. The mixed aroma of hot baked *chapati* and pungently powdered spices smelt very appetising in that late morning air.

The Delhi sun was warming up rapidly. I turned another corner and found myself before Uncle Arjun's open window. He was sitting on the floor surrounded by a scatter of photographs. Startled by my curious face at the window but recovering his poise in time, he shyly looked up and even managed to form a slow, painful smile. He nervously started fidgeting with his glasses. He took them out and brought them close to his lips. He blew on them before wiping each carefully with the edge of his loose shirt. "Er…why don't you…come…in?" It was a gentle voice that seemed to settle very comfortably amongst the cracks which criss-crossed with gay lizard abandon on his walls.

"Let me empty your ashtray first," I ventured in order to break the ice but that seemed to embarrass him even more. He got up clumsily, though, and handed it out to me. His long fingers were nicotine-stained, and yet like Dada, I noticed that his nails were neatly clipped round the edges.

As I turned around to empty the ashtray, the two little children squealed with delight. The laughter of the old woman gently admonishing them mingled wonderfully with the rhythmic grounding of the spices in the jar.

Nudged by their mischief, as it were, I climbed in with the ashtray through Uncle Arjun's window. The smile on his face which I thought would vanish at my utterly unladylike entrance, instead, broadened into a grin. This was not the same man I had seen in the morning, all hunched up and silent, before his glass of milk.

"How beautiful Lajwanti was in those days," he said quietly as he noticed my glance falling on one of the photographs of his sister. "So fond of soft materials… and…delicate things. Dada had always pampered her with clothes and...stuff...that young girls of her time liked to use, but she never had to adorn herself to look beautiful. Never. She was...she was…so confident about her beauty. If only, if only she could have been confident about her...sanity, she, she wouldn't have..." He chose his words carefully, like Dada.

Arjun Uncle stopped to light another cigarette. I knew he expected no response from me, at least not yet, so I waited for his memory to untie yet another painful knot within him. "She loved Dada. Worshipped the very ground he walked on. We were a small family, you know. It was so easy in those days to be...infected...by whatever Dada did and said. It's a little different now. Different. And Lajju, she looked even more beautiful when she abandoned all her exquisite clothes for cheap handspun *khadi*." He stopped, lost for a while. Then, nudged by buried pieces of debris, he continued. "Somehow she seemed to change. The little girl with the long luxurious plaits of hair turned into a determined...patriot... Even Dada was surprised."

He looked out of the window. Taking advantage of that pause, my eyes tried to crawl deeper and deeper into the many photographs of Lajwanti strewn on the floor. I wanted my eyes to carry them like the crumbs ants carry so diligently on their backs, especially that photograph which showed her as a corpse, wrapped in the national flag, lying on a cold flower-splashed floor. Dada's proud face was streaked with a silent and controlled mourning as he sat impassively beside her. Bhabhi's entire frame seemed to have shrunk. She looked like a bag suddenly emptied of its contents in that photograph. I wondered how Uncle Arjun's face might have looked as he clicked a few feet away from his dead sister, trapping her last presence into his lens, framed by the tears that somehow did not, or could not blur the accuracy of that scene in this cleanly taken picture.

"We were used to Dada's constant imprisonments," he suddenly began again, "but, on that awful day, when they came with the news that Dada had been lined up against a wall and...executed...Lajju had quietly got up and walked into her room. And for five years. Can you imagine? For five years she never stepped out of that room. You should have seen all the people who had entered there to try and bring her out. Mahatma Gandhi and Pandit Nehru and Vallabhbhai Patel and Maulana Azad. Yet not one of them succeeded. She would laugh, point a finger at them and accuse *them* of killing her father. It was all so sad and...all…so…horrible... Even when Dada himself walked into her room, she screamed at him, "Who is this? Who is this imposter dressed up as my father? It's a trick. It's a dirty doctor's trick. Take him away. Take him away. They shot him, and we, WE allowed him to be shot. But he lives. He lives here. Here, inside me. Take him away. Take him away. Take this imposter away."

Quietly, he started gathering up all the photographs. He looked at each one for a long, long time, before putting them away in a large brown envelope.

I had wanted to question him about the couple of films that he had made, but this was neither the time nor the place for it. I wondered if this was what he had wanted to tell me as he had stared at his glass of milk that morning on the dining table? I waited for him to say more. But he said nothing. He quietly got up and stood by the window. For a long time he stood there, looking at his vegetable garden with the envelope bearing his sister's photographs resting quietly, in his palms.

~

"Premi! Premi! Where are you?" It was Dada's voice. "Come and have lunch."

After lunch I sat opposite Dada in his large study. He had decided to take the afternoon off to be with me. There had been a change of plans and one of my friends would be arriving at 5 p.m. to pick me up. He had telephoned Dada and asked him to convey the message. "So your Dada has decided to devote this afternoon to you." When he used the word "your" it suddenly dawned on me that he was trying to resurrect, in some peculiar way, his love for his daughter through me. How unlike Lajwanti I must have appeared to him, yet I felt so moved that I didn't know how to react.

"Come, let me show you something." He opened a small door and we entered what appeared to be an unused bathroom. There was a huge unwashed bathtub in the corner. It was crammed with books, files, old letters, maps, and all sorts of memorabilia. He picked up a dusty brown packet of letters tied with a shoelace. These were letters written to Lajwanti by Mahatma Gandhi. I read a few. They were short letters, written in bold handwriting by an old man, but a wise, lovely old man. They were full of laughter and homespun wisdom. They had in them just the right kind of profundity that a young girl would understand and appreciate. It was like a father writing to his daughter, encouraging her to make her discoveries and share them with him. He called her "My darling Lajju" and always ended them with "Your Indian Mickey Mouse."

We went back to his room again. "I shall be coming to Bombay shortly," Dada told me. "Maybe I'll stay with you all for a couple of days. The court case about that Sindhi magazine has come up again. Why can't the government include Sindhi among all the other National Indian Languages? So what if only 14 per cent of the Indian population speaks the language? Sindhis have a right to that, like all the other Indian languages. They should be given equal recognition too. When will our damn government stop being so bloody Brahmanical?"

I said goodbye to Bhabhi in the kitchen and shook hands with Uncle Arjun in his garden. Only Dada had come out to see me off. He smiled and kissed me tenderly on the forehead. He didn't say anything. I was suddenly so glad that our Sindhi community of merchants had a true patriotic man like Dada on their side. I hugged Dada tightly before getting into the car. I waved back at him as the car slowly drove away from 144 Tughlaq Kutir.

America now seemed so alien, so distant to me. I was excited about Dada's forthcoming trip to our house. I would insist that he sleep only in my bed. I could always stretch out on the floor in the hall. He would need somebody to type out his articles. Must get my Olivetti down from the cupboard and practise religiously for one hour every day. I would renew not only my library card but also become a member of a couple of suburban libraries, in case, Dada needed a lot of books for references. And I could take Dada to...

The two little children ran after the car, waving and shouting and jumping in the air. The tennis-net still sagged in the evening twilight. It did not disturb me anymore.

A RECLAMATION OF THREE PARSIS

(dedicated to Chapter One of James Joyce's *Ulysses*)

"Where do you want Ahura Mazda?" Zubin roared. "Near your groin or near your heart? *Manashnee Kunashnee.*"

"Stop it," Cyrus retorted, removing last night's crusts from his eyes. "Stop polluting the morning air with a mockery of our prayers. If there is an Ahurimand, my friend, it's you. Try cleaning your soul, sometime."

"Ah, ha, Kaviraja. When did YOU last bathe? Every inch of this lighthouse stinks." Zubin put a generous foam of lather under his armpits and proceeded to shave them perversely. They were standing on the little balcony that protruded outside the lighthouse window. Both had risen early. Homi was either sleeping or involved with his usual tedious elaborate toilet rituals. After all, he was Oxford-returned.

"Why should a repeatedly failing medical student, working more assiduously as a morgue attendant, become suddenly conscious of stink?" Cyrus arrogantly demanded picking up Zubin's shaving bowl swimming with his shaven armpit hairs and the dirty lathery foam water, and flinging the contents into the surrounding dirty green waters of the Arabian Sea. "Lots of dead bodies are being dumped into this sea these days, aren't they? Besides, the rains have failed in Bombay, once again, this year. O, by the way, have you ever seen that man who collects drinking water from the sacred Parsi Bikhabehram well in his tanned buffalo-skin hide? He stinks too, my friend. His buffalo-skin hide also. But the water inside is very sweet and very pure. And it is really the water that matters, doesn't it?"

"Who cares about water now that oil has been found just off our coastal shoreline," Zubin roared, wiping the shaving blade with his towel and carefully screwing it back in the razor. "We'll have more oil to burn than they ever could, even in Ayodyha on our lord Rama's return," he shouted to the calm sea, "especially, especially, as we celebrate these days the massacre of more *masjids* and more trains set on fire all over India. O, hell, even I seem to be infected by your poetic disease."

But Cyrus was not listening. Zubin had a tendency to go on and on once he started pontificating. Cyrus would often listen to him, out of sheer amusement, and then his mind would tire and plunge gradually into his own stormy speculations, returning from time to time to lend an attentive ear to his friend's continuous verbal stream of invectives. Parsis were pretty good at mouthing them extempore. The British had taught them well.

So, they were reclaiming the land again, Cyrus sighed. If only the skyscrapers of the rich could be driven into the sea. I wonder what our Surat ancestors would say now about this new Bombay. Most of them had come in a flotilla of tiny boats and the local raja had given them generous acres of his land. They hadn't even *signed* any written deed then. Men had greater trust in the spoken words of each other those days. Now it is the slums which are being methodically driven into the sea. All a part of some written legal contract, *especially* between the slum barons and the government officials. Swines! "...but thanks to the British, my friend," Zubin's words came crashing in like waves, "and dear, generous Mrs. Tommy-de-Rum. How crotchety, chatweary, she was, my brother! O, my favorite Anglo-Indian Mumma widow, how can I ever forget her. She left me this lighthouse in her will. Can you imagine that? Me? Who had been kicked out by his own family and community? An entire lighthouse to live in. And that too, rent-free! Are you listening, you filthy verse-monger? And do you know why? *I* was that morgue attendant who had patched up her old man when they had brought him dead, all stinking with seaweed and sputum in his nostrils."

Cyrus smiled and deliberately blew his nose.

"Good God, how he stank! Rank marine smell it was. But how well I patched him up to make him appear as a presentable corpse for all those Catholic Fathers who fart in Heaven, hallowed be their hollow names. Now, that kind of sewn-up attention, well, it required more skill than your damn poetry. And it wasn't merely a question of Science or Chemistry either. No Sir! It was a skill that had, how shall I put it, a human touch. It did not have what your poetry has, that...that constant arrogance of the intellect. It came from that proud moment when the feelings of a living man get stitched up with the feelings of a dead one." Again, Cyrus smiled and this time loudly blew his nose.

"Blow all you like, *dikra*. But stop reclaiming words only from all the books you have read and step out into the world now and then. Come more often to the morgue, for instance. You will not only see but you will also smell the different ways lives come finally to an end. And I'll show you some of the interesting instruments of my trade, as well."

Cyrus picked up a stethoscope and started examining his chest.

"I remember, once I had to wash the naked corpse of a very beautiful young woman. I was so moved by the loss of all that beauty, and I swear, I never got, not even once, an erection. That would have been such an insult especially when death, in rare instances such as this, always seems to give life some unexpected kind of purity."

Cyrus coughed, now putting the doctor's instrument to his lungs.

"Poor Mrs. Tommy-de-Rum. I never knew her first name. I always called her mothermadam. And she liked that. She was so different from all those other weeping Indian mothers I have to encounter on a daily basis. Her late husband had been a lighthouse-keeper during the glorious days of the British Raj. He had kept, in his entire lifetime, all those English ships, loaded with the loot of all our Indian spices, safe from the rocks. Poor man."

"When he retired, he was left with nothing but a monthly 500-rupees pension. Rupees, mind you, not even pounds! O, those British bastards. The British, of course, had left India by then. But Her Majesty's Government still sent him that pension all the way from Buckingham Palace."

Cyprus put the stethoscope down and peered through one of Zubin's labfinders.

"Yes, sir. Five hundred rupees that arrived, every month, *par avion*, which that poor shambling relic went to collect on the first day of every month from the British Embassy that had to endorse it first. And every payday he pleaded with those Union Jack stiffjocks to get him and his wife a safe 'passage home'. And every payday they smiled, shook their shoulders, and patted him on the back, promising to put his request up to 'higher authorities'. Bastards."

Cyrus had picked up a scalpel and was starting to test its sharpness.

"One day he went mad. Stark...raving...maa-d! He ran through the Embassy corridor breaking all the glass frames. O, how I would have loved to be there. He even managed to disfigure the Queen's portrait, and not just by drawing a moustache over her stiff upper-lip, before they finally caught him and started beating him soundly. The 1857 Sepoy Mutiny had given them a lot of practice, of course, especially after his senseless figure was subsequently found, much later on a patch of deserted beach. According to the local fisherman, he had woken up, screamed an old maritime obscenity, and walked into the sea. And he had kept on walking till he drowned. Hours later they dragged him out like a prehistoric mammal..."

Cyprus gave a sudden cry. He had cut his thumb with the scalpel.

But what mammal did his own father, the honorable Pirosha Mugaseth resemble as he was masticated between the vultures' beaks at the *dakhma*? Cyrus silently sucked the blood flowing not only from his recent wound, but from all the other family induced ones.

Are Anglo Indian mothers really different from ours? O, Mumma. I can still smell the *adoo-lasan* that you could never clean from your fingers.

And did you have to curse poor Father Miranda who became my adopted father? I wanted to live my own way. Did Pirosha Mugaseth have a right to sell all of my books? And then to beat me with his billiard cue? If Father Miranda hadn't stopped him, I would have died.

When the good Father invited me to stay with him at the end of our street, I know, it was shameful for you. But not for me. They said it was I who killed you by bringing on that sudden heart attack. And now you sit on my chest, like some sort of a brooding idol demanding constant penance from me. You've been doing that for a month now, especially in my dreams. Where is that damn Band-Aid, anyway?

Now, what do you want from me, dead mother? The dead are supposed to live in their world. Go live in yours and leave me alone in mine. Your other children are looking after your property now. I'm sure they have removed all my photographs from all those family albums you spent hours with. If only I had not been your favourite son.

As the wound was bandaged, Zubin smiled at Cyrus, and advanced to the next level of his usual pontification.

"...Of what use is the lotus in a pond choked with bacteria and mosquitoes? Can you dip your filthy fingers in that pond to pluck that flower out? Hey, I'm beginning to sound like a poet too, in my middle age. O sea. No. No, O divine liquid mother, I have plucked too much of life from dead bodies and to wet them with your foam is not something I like doing. Their skins were once like the lotus too..."

Lost in his thoughts, Zubin stopped talking. He turned and slowly went down the staircase into the main room. Cyrus stood on the balcony for a long, long time. All around him, the reclamation was still going on. Like him, Zubin had been expelled from his wealthy Parsi home.

"My father," he had once told Cyrus, "wanted two obedient sons. When my mother presented him with me as a prodigal son, he threw me out. It broke her heart. She died. I was orphaned. It was as simple as that."

Cyrus felt the oppressive heat of the Bombay sun as its rays hit the sides of the lighthouse. He went down the steps slowly. Homi was still in his Oxford retreat in the bathroom. Zubin had picked him up one day, and brought him to his lighthouse, as casually as he himself had been brought by Zubin a few months earlier from the local "Auntie's joint" where all prodigal sons went to lick their wounds. Cyrus remembered Zubin telling him the night he dragged him here, "One reject has to do something for another reject, otherwise where is our *manishnee* and *gavashnee*, eh? This lighthouse shall soon become the abode of all the rejects in Bombay. After all, this building was another Mom's gift to me." Cyrus had sat down in the middle of the road and Zubin, encouraged by such attention, had pointed out, "This magnificent structure is attached to me. It is like...my *lingam*. *I* live in it. *We* live in it. And, *we* all are the supreme beings *it* shelters. Look at it. It's solid. It's strong. It's upright, and, never forget, it's always ERECT. My friend, we should be like it, or at least *try* to be like it. You say you work in a municipal school in Bandra? Yes? Good. I work in the morgue.

I talk to dead people. You, of course, talk to little children. So, we're one of a kind. Ex-spatout-patriot Parsis!"

Cyrus had laughed, and then fallen silent, waiting for the next explosion from Zubin.

"Now. Do they in turn teach you anything? I'll tell you what. The next time they give you any trouble, those little brats of yours, just bring them over to the morgue. I get a lot of dead children there too. At least twice a month. Your brats can learn a lot from them, and you too, you too, my sad-faced Parsi friend.

"The dead, you see, open the eyes of the living. Yes, those eyes that are normally shut. Now where are my damned keys? Ha. Here they are, my *chabee*s, my keys, my *chabee*s of the kingdom.

"Hey, Cyrus. Come here quickly," Zubin suddenly bawled as Cyrus came slowing into the room. "Listen. Ugh! How you stink. Listen, my lice-infested bard. We don't have much money this month. I don't expect to be paid till the 26th. Now that bourgeois bastard, Homi, has a lot of money. His old man may have kicked him out but he still maintains, discreetly of course, a bank balance in his disgraced son's name, to stop the gossip from spreading. So, please, '*chabee*' him a little, will you? And if you can't, let me. Trying out his 'social experiment' with us, is he? What do they teach him in Oxford, anyway? By staying with us 'rent-free.' You call *that* a social experiment?"

Cyrus chuckled, but said nothing.

"Now, what the hell does he do in the bathroom for so long? On the one hand I have to live with you who seldom bathes. And on the other hand, I have *him* meticulously cleaning himself every day. No wonder the

Parsi race will die out in another hundred years. But this is a question of the belly. See. Your belly and my belly. They both have to be fed. Right?" So, please *chabee*..."

...*Chabees*? My mother used to wear a bunch of keys around her waist. She carried her entire household there. All Parsi women do. Zubin carries a bunch of keys too. At the morgue I've seen him constantly locking and unlocking those long, coffin-like drawers where the corpses are kept: checking the plastic wraps; checking the temperature of the ice; fumigating, dusting...*Chabee Homi*? But what use would that be? He has never locked or unlocked anything, so far in his life.

Just then, Homi came in glistening like a porpoise. He sat down at the table and started buttering a toast. "I say, old man," he began in that patronising Oxford voice of his, "Zubin here tells me that you have a most interesting theory about Hamlet. And correct me if I'm wrong, I believe it concerns the following question—if Krishna had been chosen to advise Hamlet about his paternal dilemma at his Parsi Baug, as he once did to Prince Arjuna on the battlefield of Kurukshetra, what new version of the Gita would he have preached to our Danish born-again Parsi? I would like to listen to it sometime. You don't mind if I jot down a few of your observations, do you?"

Before the sneer became too pronounced on Cyrus' face, Zubin jumped in. "My two much-ado-about-nothing Parsi gentlemen, Krishna would have begun by first playing the flute and teaching Hamlet *bawa* not to be played upon. Then, he would proceed, let me see, ah, yes, to seduce all the Baug's buxom and flat-chested Parsi *doodhwalis* besides their grunting Amul cows, so that they would increase and multiply, increase and multiply the *rottenness* in the Baug, of course, with new versions of *ghee* and glee...and...

"Then, and then, when poor Zenobia came looking for tulsi, rosemary and thyme, he would waylay her with his *bansuri* and pierce, ever so gently, ever so urgently, with an *ashem vohu* gentleness, her divinehead with his *'tool.'* And our untouched Zenobia would *come* and *come*, crushing all her roses and all her Maries (like all Parsis she was very cosmopolitan, especially in her choice of religions) on her breasts, while poor princess Mira would seethe with Rajput fury as she waited for her lord in her fort. And then, while Hamlet *bawa* was sharpening *his* other tool for his duel with her brother Rustom, Krishna would quickly steal into Zenobia's mother, Lady Coover's closet and start making passionate love to her, yes, right there in the dark, this time with that old fool Kawassa watching from behind the *machhardani*, as Krishna wooed and murmured into her ears, 'I am the *other* Kawas, come back from Homi Wadia's studio to reclaim you, my love. Fix your eyes only upon me as Nadiya would have and surrender.' She wouldn't know the difference in the dark, anyway, for like all Indian mothers, Lady Coover was shortsighted anyway. Ask Cyrus here. *His* mother plays a very important role in his interpretation of the play too, doesn't she?"

"How dare you insult my Momma," Cyrus responded, rising from the table where he had been seated. "And how dare you insult the very idea of MOTHER! I shall not allow her, even though she is dead, to be insulted by a...a... mere keeper of corpses assuming the position of a pot-bellied Hamlet."

"Didn't your Mrs. Tommy-de-Rum treat you like a son? Was that *shortsighted* of her, you ungrateful bag of wind? Stay out of my family courtyard you hear. You have your own to deal with. Go trumpet your theories there. Don't you ever..."

There was a knock at the door which Cyrus angrily wrenched open. It was the old Parsi rag-and-bone woman. She came every third day to collect old bottles, torn slippers, rags, anything that she could sell for a pittance to survive in her day-to-day precarious existence, now that the sanatorium had thrown her out.

"O, Mother India! O, Divine Mother! What have you come to take from us now?" shouted Zubin, prostrating himself before her, and touching her feet in mock gestures of respect. The old woman, perspiring, stinking and demented by a string of her own families' betrayals, grinned through her toothless mouth, not understanding a word of what Zubin was saying but perversely enjoying all the attention he was giving her.

"...Ooo, that pig. He will never learn. Poor woman. Like Momma, she smells of *adoo-lasan* too."

Old woman. Who will be called to collect your remains? Do you have a husband? Do you have a son? A daughter? Are they all dead? Did they leave you, as they normally do, one by one? That's the lot of Indian mothers. If they only could say NO at *that* time, yes, that crucial time. But no. That word was never written in their destinies. I wish I could have made you understand, Mother. I wish...

Cyrus closed the door and got slapped harshly by the sun. He staggered for a moment before groping for the nearest rock and squatted on it. He took out snot from his nose and pasted it on the rock. He looked back through the open door... Somebody must have opened it after him. Was it Gandhi, or was it Nehru, who used the word 'usurper?' O God, what's the use. They are reclaiming the land again. "Jana Gana Mana Adhinayaka Jaya He, Bharata Bhagya Vidhata." Ah, Tagorebabu, India's supreme poetkavi. Would those words of your National Anthem for this...this India of ours still profess to say to-day, "Thou Art the Ruler of All Thy People, Thou Dispenser of India's Destiny?"

Poor, poor Nehru. On the day of Independence, he had proclaimed, "India has a tryst with destiny." Words. Mere words. What prehistoric monsters and mammals will this generation that is yet to come after us produce for all those people who are dying to come and occupy this reclaimed land? We *are* in a land of usurpers. Yes, each and every one of us. He got up and slowly started walking towards his school.

"Cyrus. Hey, Cyrus. O, poetkavi. Come back...Can you hear me? You have forgotten your keys. Your *chabee*s! Hey..."

But Cyrus walked on till Zubin's voice got drowned by the roar of the waves in their monotonous race against the rocks. The children would be waiting for him. Waiting and grinning like prehistoric monsters! He stopped and stared at the water as in the distance, the reclamation went calmly on.

THE FUSS ABOUT QUEENS

As a small boy, he had been punished for deliberately removing the framed photograph of Queen Victoria and smashing it on the floor. Now, as Gieve sat in the corner of his room, studying on the eve of his Master's exam in Political Science, Dubash Building was going progressively mad as it got ready to cheer Queen Elizabeth II during her maiden appearance in the city of Bombay.

The epidemic had started the previous evening.

The madness began where their dirty lane, sandwiched between the Bohri restaurant kitchen and the *mootri*—piss wall—began. Tyabjee, the owner of the restaurant, *The* Grand Oriental, was getting many of his menu boards repainted. Instead of Mughlai chicken, Gieve watched the painter imprint 'Chicken Fit for a Queen'. Even dessert-like drinks, Gieve noticed, were rapidly changing their gender. The restaurant's most popular 'Badshah Faluda' was now 'Rani Faluda.'

As Gieve walked up to talk to Tyabjee about these changes, the latter respectfully brushed him aside. "No time for politics today, Gieve *beta*. I'm very, very busy. I have to label a lot of these new beer bottles. They have just arrived from Ulhasnagar. Have you drunk this new beer? It's called 'Windsor Beer'. Try it. Try it. It's a drink fit..."

"...fit for a queen. I know, I know, Tyabjee," Gieve laughed.

Tyabjee smiled and winked at Gieve. "God bless Her Majesty. Business has trebled since she first set foot in our Bombay."

The queen seemed to have infected even Haaji Mastaan, Dubash Building lane's self-appointed *diwana* muralist. Gieve had spent hours admiring this self-taught artist's weekly creations on the wall. Haaji Mastaan's fame, however, did not merely rest on his murals. In his own way, he had magically solved the building residents' problem—an overwhelming urinary stench—all within the space of just one night and one day.

If you stayed in Dubash Building, you had to confront two distinct odours. The first was that emanating from Mrs. Mascarenas' Auntie's Joint and her local distillery. At times, this smell was overcome by the more agreeable one of Golden Wafers, especially when enormous quantities of potatoes were boiled and fried and cut into thin *salli* or what Parsis recently returned from the US of A called French fries. But the most unbearable was that urine stench when most of Mrs. Mascaranas' drunken customers stumbled out of her joint and headed for the wall across the lane with alarming regularity in order to relieve themselves.

It was Haaji Mastaan who had finally come to the rescue of the lane's long-suffering residents. Since he slept in a tiny improvised tin-shed that he had constructed ingeniously out of caste-off Glucose biscuit tins, often donated to him by the restaurant's resident cook, he too was tired of this regularly mapped-out urinary universe around him. Gathering his latest collection of coloured chalks that the obliging residents of Dubash Building constantly supplied him with, he spent an entire night and day cleaning that offensive wall, first whitewashing it thoroughly, and then dexterously painting on its inviting canvas the powerful images of a forgiving Jesus Christ, a tolerant Gautama Buddha, a militant grimfaced Rama, an angrily aroused Shiva, and an I-told-you-so mocking Krishna. Haaji Mastaan, however, left a prominent blank space close to his tin-shed dwelling, and people had started taking wagers to see whose portrait would finally fill that up.

Ever since these painted figures appeared as the lane's newly housed tenants, the daily wayward pissers, as though obeying the dictates of all the painted gods' collective gazes, completely stopped their nocturnal ritual. No matter how drunk any *sharabi* felt, those gods on the wall exercised such a sober influence on their kidneys that they had to seek other avenues for moonshine *moksha*.

As Gieve walked into the lane, he suddenly stopped in his tracks. There was Haaji Mastaan applying the finishing touches to his brand new and most recent portrait in that space that had stood empty for so many months—Queen Elizabeth II. "There Gieve baba," beamed Haaji Mastaan, "ours is the most unique gully in the whole of Bombay. It has five *bhagwans* and one *firangi* rani."

The queen's motorcade, as reported by the newspapers, was expected to pass by Dubash Building at noon. It would arrive from Bombay Central and make its way all along the length of Grant Road's Lamington Road. Why the queen was interested in making her way down this old road where once English theatre companies had thrived and flourished in the triumphant days of the Raj naturally aroused Gieve's historical curiosity. "I always thought," he told his parents, "that the queen was more interested in horses, horse-races, jockeys, you know, four-legged breeding, and would rather have spent this Sunday afternoon with trainers and riders at the Royal Turf Club at Mahalakshmi instead of creating all this *nutkhut tamasha.*"

His father, who was ironing an old gabardine suit he intended to wear when he would wave at the queen from his balcony, snapped back at Gieve. "*You* have a jockey imagination, *bacchu*. Try and rise for once above your usual nonsense-bred nationalism and all that damn Marxist rubbish they are teaching you at university these days."

Kekobad Faramroz Mistry—although he lived with his son Gieve and wife Freny in Dubash Building, in a third-floor *chawl,* whose three rooms were horizontally constructed like a cabin in an ocean liner, and although he made a comfortable living by being the sole owner of The Hampton Court Ice Factory which was started by his father Piroshah in a 50-50 partnership with an Englishman, Sebastian Outram, Kekobad was in no mood, especially on this auspicious Union Jack day, to tolerate any *desi* dissent from his anarchic Anglo-Indian Parsi *dikroo*.

As usual, just before a heated argument broke out between her husband and her son, Freny hastily retreated into the comfortable space of her kitchen. That was the only place where *she* felt like a queen! She had woken up very early today. A lot of cooking had to be done in celebration of 'our *rani*'. First, she had swept and swabbed the floors of her three rooms. Her Gangabai, who usually did these tasks, was asked not to come in because she was in her unclean menstrual period. Freny did not want any pollution in her home today. Today belonged exclusively to her *rani*. After all, the *rani*'s car would pass right under her balcony. If *only* the *rani* would look up, catch her eye, and smile at her.

Excitement of this kind was very rare and hard to come by in her normal invisible life. Today, somehow, she felt peculiarly energised as she decorated the entrance to her house with *rangoli* on the floor. It didn't matter if the English signs of WELCOME had got mixed up with the Parsi ones of SAAL MUBARAK. They both *meant* the same thing. Pausing to review her work, she suddenly had an idea. Quickly filling coloured powder into an empty Flit insecticide pump, she spelt out in her neat, tiny hand in the middle of her door—GOD SAVE THE QUEEN.

Muzzafar Mian, the *muttonwala*, had been carefully instructed by her to get the best *tukda* of lamb for today. "No icegosht, *muaa*," she had thundered at him. "I want to see blood dripping on the mutton, you hear."

Muzzafar Mian had been delivering mutton to Frenybai for the past 20 years, ever since Gieve *baba* had been born. He was known for cheating his other Dubash Building customers, usually in small, tolerable ways, but never his Frenybai. To him, she was 'Dubash Building *ki rani*'. Muzzarfar Mian entrusted everything to her. Since he was illiterate, she had even opened a bank account for him. Every time he had to deposit or withdraw money, she went along with him to the bank and conducted business on his behalf.

When Muzzafar Mian had shocked the building by announcing his second marriage to an 18-year-old cousin (who had actually come to visit Bombay), it was Frenybai who had gone with him to make peace, not only with his whole *mohalla*, but also with his first *begum*. So good had Frenybai been that she had even persuaded Muzzafar Mian's first *begum* to not only choose the wedding trousseau but to also part with some of her jewels for her younger connubial rival.

Family quarrels between her husband and son, however, Freny could never handle because they always erupted over 'politics,' especially of the 'Raj'.

So she quietly closed the door to her kitchen and concentrated on boiling the vermicelli, raisins, and almonds that she would later serve with boiled eggs for breakfast to her two men. This was the Parsi way of inaugurating festive occasions. Perhaps it would sweeten them up.

She lifted the icebox lid. There was plenty of chilled beer in there. "Hé Zarathustra," she sighed to herself. "Hope all my cooking *piglofies* them a bit."

Indeed, her trump card lay in her splendid *dhandar-patya* and *tareli mucchi* which was slowly getting ready on the Criterion *choola*. That heavy lunch, she hoped, would make husband and son amicable again. "Who knows, they might even fall into each other's arms by the evening. After all, they should make some concessions for our *rani*. If only our *rani* could taste my delicacies." She was sure no one in Buckingham Palace, or even in all the Indian restaurants in all of London, could cook like her.

As she started stirring the food, she wondered if her husband and son would continue to bicker if the *rani* impulsively stepped out of her car and insisted on having lunch with them. She remembered Gandhi*ji* doing that. Didn't he stay with the *bhangi*s at Dongri rather than with the Birlas at Cumbhalla Hill? For Freny, Gandhi and Elizabeth II, were both stewed in the same cooking pot of history. Things were not so simple and amicable, unfortunately, on the other side of her kitchen door.

"So," Kekobad fired the opening salvo, "what *satyagraha* are you planning, today, *bacchu*?"

"Nothing remarkable," Gieve countered. "Between 12 and, let me see, 12.30, that is, between two chimes of our trusty Big Ben clock, there will be one person in Dubash Building who will refuse to get up from his study-table to cheer for your queen and for Mom's *rani*."

Now that the ice was broken, or as old Mrs. Mascarenas, their feisty old Goan neighbour, would say, "Now that the *billi* was out of the *thayli*", Kekobad settled his corpulent self deep down in his favourite easy chair. It was going to be a protracted argument and he was determined to get the better of his educated son as a mark of loyalty to his queen.

"I guess that will make you some kind of a hero, eh? A little *badshah*! Maybe one of your journalist friends will write a little sketch about Grant Road's one and only Indian patriot. Now, our Parsi newspaper, the *Jam-e-Jamshed, of course*, won't report on your anti-*angrezi* stand. We Parsis got along very well with the British, you know, and the editor, God bless him, still gives me lots of space for my Hampton Court Ice Factory ads at the old rates."

Gieve smiled. "Of course it won't, Puppa. *Jam-e-Jamshed*'s Parsi editor is a confirmed Anglophile. Just like you. You know, his reputation was built on all those farcical Parsi theatrical productions of Oscar Wilde's plays he regularly produces. What is he currently producing? O yes, *The Importance of Being Ernest*. He has even directed it himself. Have you seen it? It's on at the Tejpal Auditorium. You must see it for its atrocious mediocrity. God! How the Parsis of Bombay lap it all up."

Kekobad stuffed his pipe with one of the latest imported British tobacco brands, and put his feet up on the table. As he inspected the fine job he had done in ironing his trouser creases, he continued, "Ah. The importance of being earnest *is* really the question confronting us in India, isn't it, *bacchu*? Being earnest to our Indian leaders has not really brought us any prosperity or peace of mind, has it?"

"No, it hasn't," replied Gieve putting *his* feet up on the study desk in mock imitation of his father. "But that is because *you* don't want to see your country with your own eyes. The difference between your attitude to our history and mine is very simple, Puppa."

"In our school, for instance, we were forced to study Indian History written only by British historians like Father Gense or Henry Rawlinson. We were forced to acknowledge a colonial way of coming to terms with our past, our present, and our future. I remember how angry my History teacher got when I cited an Indian historian, Ishwari Prasad's reference in my paper on the Indian Mutiny of 1857. It was as if *I* had been mutinous myself."

"To day, our teachers are only trying to make us read our country's history though several ignored Indian sources, official and non-official. In a way, they are opening Indian eyes that have been closed for so long, or those superimposed, like yours, with English lenses."

"Look at him," Kekobad gesticulated, "giving *me* a lecture on Indian History, and that too in the ENGLISH *bhasha*! Whose language is that, *bacchu*?"

"It is theirs, Puppa," Gieve conceded, "but the thought is not. The thought is Indian. And it should always be Indian. And if the English language can be used to convey all Indian thoughts convincingly, then all the better for it. But why this absurd *tamasha* over Queen Elizabeth? I am sure she is a very nice lady. But why all this Raj revivalism? If we really want to venerate *ranis* and queens then why not any of our own? Why don't we celebrate Rani Lakshmibai's great *qurbani* for the Indian cause or Rani Jeejabai's wise counsels to her son, Shivaji? Sohrab Modi did make a very bad film, *Jhansi Ki Rani,* but at least he was one Parsi, unlike our *Jam-e-Jamshed* editor, who chose a proper Indian subject to canonise."

That didn't wash with Kekobad. Shifting gears, he blandly inquired, "How would you explain Nehru's infatuation with Edwina Mountbatten, then? She was a queen in his life too, wasn't she?"

"In the same way as you drink Bombay Gin and then toast Queen Victoria's label on the bottle, or President Mohammed Ali Jinnah marrying a Bombay Parsi millionaire's daughter and then surprising all Indians, especially the Parsis, by creating Pakistan. The next thing you'll want to know is how come Gandhi*ji* was killed by a *saffron* Hindu and not a *green* Muslim or a *white* Englishman? It's a question of ideology, and ideology is hard to explain to an old diehard like you. It's not like making ice; first freezing it with proper chemicals and then shaping it under the right pressure. Ideology is like water. It flows and you have to be swept away by it, you have..."

"So father and son are at it again about the *purana firangi Hindustani jhagda*, eh?" Old Mrs. Mascarenas now hobbled into the room to return the previous day's newspaper. "Why do you two *bachhas* make so much fuss about politics? Hindustani, *firangi,* what's the difference, men? I lost my Hindustani husband and my *nashatani* eldest son to *narangi* hooch. Even then, my younger sons make it, drink it, and I, their mother, sell it. Yes, especially to those *chee chee goras* who did not return to *vilayat*. This is, don't you see, my only pension, *re*.

"There is good and there is bad in every period of one's life. Accept it and learn to live with it. Take your ice-factory, Kekoo. Isn't it running solely on a 50-50 *Hindustani firangi kismat*? Now, if you took away one 50, would the other 50 survive? It wouldn't. Then why are you constantly fighting?

"I've been listening to both of you for the last half an hour, and even though I'm deaf in one ear, I've managed to hear enough. If our Gieve baba doesn't want to wave at your *rani*, why are you forcing him, Kekoo? *You* wave!

"My, my. That gabardine suit sure looks nice on you still. Like your boy, a lot of my hooch workers won't be waving at the *rani* either. And why should they? What should I tell my daily *grahak*? Sorry, boys, no *daru* today in honour of the queen?"

"Let the boy study instead. He's got his final paper tomorrow. Won't you be proud when he gets his First Class, as he has been getting all these years? Then when you distribute *mithai* to the whole building, will you be thinking of Her Majesty, Queen Elizabeth II?"

"Now, where is today's paper? I want to see what that fat Bejan has to say about my lean fortune today."

Hearing Mrs. Mascarenas, Freny quickly entered the room with three bowls of delicious vermicelli. "You think the queen will be wearing pink today, Mrs. Mascarenas?"

"Well, that depends, Freny darling," the old lady replied shrewdly, "on whether she's *in* the pink and whether *we*, her public, are in the pink as well. Now, are we?"

Gieve took his vermicelli bowl and retreated into his room, closing the door behind him. Kekobad cleared his throat and left the room hurriedly to fetch the old lady her newspaper. The two women looked at each other and suddenly burst into a peal of laughter.

And as the Big Ben clock chimed the hour, the two queens strolled out to the balcony, arm in arm, to wait for their *rani* to arrive.

IT TAKES TWO TO BHAGDIG

"How on earth did a Parsi like you get the name of Bijlikhan?"

For a moment I was stunned. Firstly, persistent doorbells chiming at 8.30 in the a.m. and that too on a Sunday morning makes you grind your teeth at the sudden invasion of your privacy. On top of that to have your own pedigree questioned so rudely, and that too by a complete stranger!

"My great great grandfather," I sneered at the stranger standing at my door, "ran away with a dancing girl called Bijli and then fought a deadly duel with her enraged lover, Khan, on the banks of the river Sutlej."

"No need to descend on me like *bijli*, dear professor. May I come in? Thank you."

There seemed to be something determined, something compulsive behind all that resplendent corpulence that brushed past one and settled comfortably in my living room. There was insolence too, but it was not calculated. Rather, it was infectious and, in a strange way attractively challenging. He meandered towards the nearest comfortable chair and descended slowly into it.

"I've just had," he began nonchalantly, as though I was an old, old friend, "an excellent plate of brown bread and *maska*, Professor, and when you dip it in that specially *doodhified* Iranian *chai*, the taste of last night's hangover is completely gone and the memory of all that cheap perfume gets lost completely in the aroma of this wonderfully brewed tea."

"My dear sir," I replied, trying very hard not to burst any more blood vessels, "I do not need your hack poetry about Sunday morning breakfasts or Saturday night leftovers in Bombay. If you happen to have fathered a wayward son or an insolent daughter now urgently needing English tuitions at the 11th hour, forget it. And I don't know any corrupt clerks in the Bombay University either who could sell you question papers for the upcoming exams for a negotiable price. Indian parents of duffers seem to suddenly wake up when the exams are just around the corner. I've had enough with the damn Indian academic system and...what is *your* name and what, for God's sake, do you mean by this rude *itvaar* intrusion?"

"You'd better sit down too, Professor. And stop putting the tonga before the *ghoda*. I call myself Bhagdig and—"

I snorted loudly and rudely like a tonga horse! "What do you mean you *call* yourself Bhagdig? Is it an acronym or something?"

"There you go again," he replied nonchalantly, not in the least offended by all of *my* explicit digs! "You must be, I'm quite sure Professor, one of those writers who regularly figure in the *Times of India* 'middles' on the editorial page. You certainly sound like one. Sir, I don't know what an acronym is, and I don't want to." As I rose up to protest, he hushed me down.

"Hold on, hold on, before you lapse into another one of your Wren & Martin speeches. See, I remember my grammar book from my English classes. I'm a private detective and I think I *know* who has the rare first edition of the Raymond Chandler Omnibus of the Complete Philip Marlowe novels. It has been…er…*missing* from the J.V. Saklatvalla Library for over a month now."

I did sit down, but with a certain amount of outraged dignity. Now it was my turn to enjoy *my* cup of tea. I took my time stirring it, till the pleasant scent of the mint leaves and the lemongrass soaking in the tea filled the entire room. It was also to make him aware that as a Parsi I too took my tea drinking very seriously.

"And how," I began, "did the famous detective Bhagdig deduce that? And that too on a Sunday morning, when most of Bombay's Roman Catholics are at church, her Muslims at the *masjid*, her Hindus at the *mandir*, and most, barring *some* of her Parsis, at the *agyari*? In simple Wren & Martin English, my dear fellow, when people are doing decent God-fearing things on Sunday mornings, why are you putting such an indecent allegation on a former, well-respected professor of English Literature from what used to be one of our finest colleges, the—"

"Loyola College. I know that Professor. I know that. I've done my homework. Boy," he continued, helping himself to another cup of my mint tea, "you sure have a way of pouring forth your views instead of just putting them simply across. Thank God I'm only a matric-pass. Tell me, Professor, did you ever finish your teaching syllabus in time? I bet you called your poor groaning students for extra lectures on weekends, especially Sundays? No?"

He was close, dangerously close to shattering the famous Bijlikhan mercury. "If you don't leave here this instant, my dear man. I'll really make you *bhag*. I'm not one of those easy-chair college professors, you know. And stop pushing your nose into other people's affairs. And by the way, that's not a very good name you've coined for yourself."

"It's appropriate Professor, and, you must admit, a little unusual," he explained casually, suddenly summoning up a lot of pride. "I get half my clients that way. Besides, it's a definite improvement over Bhagwat, which is my real name, and it sums up my profession very well. But there's no need for *you* to get so upset. If you asked me, rare books that nobody ever bothers to read in our libraries *deserve* to be stolen. They get eaten up by white ants, anyway."

I was quite surprised by that casually offered, but accurate observation. Most people have a method in their madness. This man had madness in his method and he continued to display it for my benefit. After all, I *was* to him, still, the alleged *thief*.

"It wasn't difficult, as you pointed out, Professor, to deduce who could have stolen *that* rare book. You see, in the last 10 years, the only person who had consistently taken out that volume from the library was *yourself*. There had been a few others, but they had returned it almost immediately and never bothered to check it out again. On the other hand, you seemed to pour over it, sometimes over a period of three to four months, till, I'm sure, one day, the temptation to possess it and save you all this trouble of borrowing it once again must have really overcome you."

I poured myself a stiff bracer of tea and started stirring it, clockwise for a change. "You must be joking, Bhagdig," I replied calmly. "Even if I stole it, how on earth are you going to prove it? Do you have any witnesses? It'll basically be your word against mine. And professors, my dear man, do claim a much higher priority in the courtroom than detectives, right?"

He smiled and unbuttoned his shirt's top button, little realising, that his shirt still looked crooked having been buttoned the wrong way in the first place. I had a great temptation to point that out to him, but something stopped me. Something told me that even if I did, he wouldn't bother to straighten out his shirt. He was that kind of man. He could see civility even in a carelessly tied shoe string. And I confess, I like that kind of a man. "Look, Professor, I'm not here to threaten you with any impending arrest. Actually, I need your cooperation for… er…a delicate scheme of mine."

"And what if I don't go along with whatever hare-brained scheme you have in mind?" I enquired.

"Well, then you'll force me to er...pursue the stolen angle, Professor," he replied, now munching on a macaroon. "You may not know any corrupt clerks in Bombay University, but I do know a lot of crooked lawyers in the Bombay High Court compound who are willing to write out an arrest summons at the mere snap of my finger. Now you wouldn't like that, would you, Professor? And I know a lot of reporter cronies too in the Bombay Press Club. A few words from me, carelessly slipped out, of course, over drinks, could make the future very uncomfortable for you, wouldn't it? After all, I *have* been hired by old

Saklatvalla himself to recover that lost volume. Besides, it's not merely a book. It's a family heirloom."

"If it is a family heirloom," I demanded, "then what may I ask was it doing on the library's shelf, along with all the other books, in the first place?"

"That's an interesting question, Professor," he said, now consuming his fourth macaroon in between sips from his third cup of tea. "It has something to do with, if you'll pardon me, a certain kind of Parsi pettiness which usually comes out only when some sort of absurd rivalry is about to be established. Not the open hostile kind, which is characteristic of most of our other Indian communities, but rather of a quiet subtle type that is often more painful. I often seem to find it in a lot of Parsi homes. Over the years I have visited quite a few, Professor. I've had lots of Parsi clients. I know your community quite well. For instance, I see this quiet hostility most commonly between a brother and a sister, a parent and a child, an uncle and a nephew...it's not *that* infectious amongst Parsi husbands and wives, though, thank God...

Now, these Parsi *lok* will stay for years in the same house without once ever speaking to each other. Not even on your Navroze and Papeti days. And although they will help each other and look after each other on a daily basis, not one kind word or one affectionate gesture will ever be exchanged between them. Strange, isn't it, Professor, especially when this sort of thing happens even in the most cultured homes of your community. It seems to me that your entire *qaum*, I'm afraid to say, hasn't advanced from Nausari at all. Ah, these macaroons are very good indeed. Are they from Nausari?"

"No Mister Bhagdig," I replied, stung at this overwhelming assault on my community. "They're from Poona's Kayani Bakery. "

"Oh, I'm terribly sorry, Professor," he said. "I wasn't trying to get personal or communal. I was just trying to explain this…this extraordinary Parsi estrangement that also occurred between Old Saklatvalla and his father, Maneckshaw. He always spelt the last part of his name like an Englishman, with a 'w'."

"I believe you," I snapped back, a little gruffly, "and stop calling me Professor. I retired 10 years ago. The name's Sam. And I like to pronounce it as the Americans do, and not Sssaam as the Parsis do."

"Or psalm, as the Christians do?" he enquired. We both laughed. "Names are funny things," he resumed in a quiet voice. "Somehow there are very few people whom I can really call by their first names. Right now, Professor seems to suit you so I hope you won't mind, Sam? Maybe it's because I grew up in a neighbourhood where before one could actually feel the pride of one's first name, one's last name somehow always managed to disgrace it. *That* is the kind of world I come from, Professor." He lapsed into silence, leaving me confronting a peculiar area of grace where I could observe him.

There was no denying it. I liked this outrageous intrusion that he had made into my life this Sunday morning. I could feel a strange kind of excitement, the last of which I had felt many many years ago when...but this was neither the time nor the place to fall back on such useless nostalgia. Retirement had brought to my life, not the anticipated peace I thought it would, but rather the tedium of having to live one's day like the remorseless ticking of the clock that refuses to go faster or slower than the correctness of the hour and the exactness of the minutes, the seconds it is expected to uphold. I secretly hated my correctness, my regularity, my time-tabled movements during *all* seven days of the week.

Now with Bhagdig, I suddenly glimpsed a door I could slip through. A vision of anarchy seemed to swell up in my breast, and for the first time I felt a complete lack of resistance in myself to stop it. There sat Bhagwat, alias Bhagdig, with his lopsided shirt eating my macaroons avidly with the same fingers with which, in between mouthfuls, he peeled off enormous layers of epidermis from his horribly misshapen toes.

"Ugly, aren't they," he admitted, quick to notice my gaze and my winces every time he peeled off yet another patch of skin. "It seems all the Bhagwats in the family do it."

"Could we please get back to the Saklatvalla case, Bhagdig," I interrupted him. "I don't find peeling skin stories palatable, especially on a Sunday morning."

"O, all right, Professor. One likes to occasionally climb up one's family tree. I doubt whether Saklatvalla would agree with me on that. He and his father, Maneckshaw, never spoke to each other for the last 15 years. Incredible isn't it?

"Now Maneckshaw, whatever his faults, was certainly a man of breeding. He had rather strange tastes for a Parsi, Professor. On the one hand he was an ardent theosophist, a member of the Blavatsky Masonic Lodge. Even today, I believe they hold fortnightly séances in an abandoned old British bungalow in the nearby hill station of Lonavla. Yet, such a man was also at home, ahem, in certain places which...er...I'm sure you must have never visited, but you well, can understand, at Forrest Road or..."

"You mean our city's famous brothels, don't you?" I asked with a little sanctimonious tone in my voice. "Yes, I understand, and don't start moralising about prostitutes now. Stick to the tale."

"You must admit, Professor, it's hard to find someone like you who is so much at ease both amongst the sacred and the profane. Well, to get back to my story, his son definitely resented it, and made no bones about it. Hence their constant squabbling till this detective fellow in the book, this this..."

"Marlowe," I said helping him out, "Philip Marlowe. The same as it was a couple of minutes ago."

Bhagdig's macaroon suddenly slipped and fell into his tea. "I beg your pardon, Professor?"

"Don't. I'm merely quoting." I liked pulling his leg now and then. It was the old habit of the professor, although digs like that was really hitting way below the belt.

"Oh, oh, I see. Well, this Marlowe chap became the central actor of this strange, this absurd insulting drama inaugurated by the old man to get back at the son, the moment the latter cut off all communication with hi—"

"Would you mind, not telling me the story backwards, Bhagdig? I prefer a story which, as good old Aristotle insisted, must have a beginning, a middle, and an end."

Bhagdig gave the spirit of poor Aristotle a very dirty look before expounding on one of the craziest narrative I had ever heard.

"Let me first explain *how* that precious volume *entered* the Saklatvalla household. The publisher of that precious volume, first presented it to Maneckshaw when the latter went to England to attend the Blavatsky anniversary celebrations. Both those men, coincidentally, seemed to have similar tastes in a lot of things. You know, the sacred and the profane? Now, not only did the old man devour the Marlowe stories but he made this, this detective chap into the kind of *symbolic son* he would have liked to have. So when he came back from England, he set up this Marlowe fellow in the Saklatvalla household as a conspicuous role model and used *him*, unfortunately, to heap insults on poor Saklatvalla.

"Although they were not on speaking terms, Maneckshaw always made it a point to read aloud to his wife and son on the dining table certain passages from the stories and then spout out, extempore, mind you, on Marlowe's incredible conduct, his bravery, his courage, etc., etc., which I'm sure, Professor, *you* would have enjoyed a great deal, had you been invited at their table. Of course ,the darts were always aimed shrewdly and cleverly at his trembling son, and poor Saklatvalla took them, I guess, as best as he could.

"Now you can imagine the *hatred* he slowly developed, not only for his father but also for *this* particular volume and *that* Marlowe fellow. You can see it even today when he talks about it. He's really a very mild and meek old Parsi, but mention that volume or utter that word 'Marlowe' and he becomes someone else."

"Well, we Parsis certainly indulged in Victorian father-son rivalries, Bhagdig, but *this* is really an extreme example. To actually, actually, resurrect a fictitious American detective, and make him into this kind of an emblem..." It was a fascinating thought I was trying to pursue, but Bhagdig soon brought me down from my pulpit, and I admit, this time he did it without any wisecracks.

"Professor," he reminded me gently, "to your humble friend Bhagdig, only the rivalry matters, and not all this fancy thinking you, I'm sure, can enlighten me with. That's why I'm a detective. You see, in my profession, I have to understand people's baser emotions in order to arrive at workable solutions. The profounder emotions are your department. So may I proceed with the tale?"

"Thank you. Now listen carefully. It gets even *more* interesting with the son's retaliation. Saklatvalla made Maneckshaw pay for all those humiliating moments. O yes, he did! And how! All those excesses of Maneckshaw's, you know, what we call, let me see, appetites, finally took their physical toll, Professor, and in his approaching old age, he became a very sick man, often confined to long periods in bed. It was then that Saklatvalla took hold of that spell of good luck, and found a clever way, yes sir, a very clever way of paying his father back. Did you, for instance, Professor, ever notice the texture of the pages of that volume?"

"Now that you mention it, Bhagdig," I suddenly remembered. "I did. It…it seemed as though somebody used to scribble a lot on them in pencil and then erase them. The pages did seem successively worn out every time I borrowed that volume. Now what on earth did Maneckshaw, or was it, Saklatvalla, write on them?"

"You guessed both wrong and right, Professor. It was Saklatvalla all right who wrote on those pages. And do you know what he wrote?"

I shook my head.

"All sorts of insulting messages like the ones you find…er…written on bathroom walls and college desks. He would underline certain passages and then write very crude and vulgar versions of them in the book's margins where he deliberately made excessive fun of *both*, that Marlowe chap *and* his father. Then he'd place that volume besides his father's sick bed. The old man, of course, was too feeble to retaliate after he read them, and his poor wife was helpless. She tried very hard to hide the book, but both men would insist on reading it, every single day."

"But this is monstrous," I exploded. "How can two educated, civilised people behave like this? It's childish. Besides, it's, it's, disgraceful."

"In spite of all your academic knowledge, Professor, you're still innocent when it comes to matters of the human heart. The heart has a logic very different from the mind, Professor. I'm sure even your Aristotle knew that the old man who had repeatedly humiliated his son's manhood, especially in the latter's youth, now found the same treatment returned to him in his feeble old age."

"He died very soon, and I'm sure that *that* volume had a big part to play in his death. Naturally, Saklatvalla wanted to get rid of that offensive book, especially from the family courtyard, so he included it, in spite of all its value with all the other detective books on his common, readily available library shelf. That way, at least, it was out of his house and his life."

"But," I pointed out to Bhagdig, "isn't he finally relieved that that offensive book has been finally stolen?"

Bhagdig chuckled. "That occurred to me also, Professor, but human nature is, in a very peculiar way, very very strange. *Now*, old Saklatvalla feels very guilty about its sudden loss. So, he wants that volume *found*. He doesn't want it to be in the possession of someone *else*. He wants, in a way, to have the satisfaction of seeing the thief caught and punished."

"As though that would excuse him from his own conduct towards his father," I expostulated. "It's better if the book remains with someone who at least knows its true value."

"Exactly Professor," Bhagdig agreed. "Exactly! But as I'm employed by him, I want to play along with this agreement and maybe in the bargain, get him to finance *my* first visit to Los Angeles and back."

Now, it was my turn to say, "I beg your pardon." What kind of a cockeyed deal was his crafty brain working on now, I wondered? And why on earth did he have to pick LA? I wasn't thinking very clearly, otherwise I should have been able to make the connection to LA quite easily. But then I was merely an ex-professor. *He* was the detective. *He* was supposed to make all the 'connections' as good old E.M. Forster insisted all humans should make.

So, I let him.

"At first," waxed my eloquent friend, "I weighed the consequences of how *I* should be benefited from this case. After all, Professor, it *is* my bread and butter. Could I get something, I asked myself, out of that man who actually *stole* that rare volume or my employer who wanted it back so desperately? But then I said to myself, how much money could the former have anyway since he had to resort to stealing in the first place. The latter, however, owned an entire library and was known to be loaded. So why not exploit Mr. Money-bags Saklatvalla himself."

"Money-bags, eh!" I couldn't help retaliating. "You know, you inspire me, you really do. I should get into your detective racket myself."

He laughed. "Spoken like an *asli* Parsi, Professor. We can be a good team you know—Bhagdig and Bijlikhan. After all it takes *two* to Bhag Dig!"

Now I was really warming up. "This is getting nicer and nicer. Tell me all about this juicy plan of yours for going to LA. And don't worry about your agency. I'll look after it in your temporary absence."

A little startled by my sudden enthusiasm, and a little suspicious of whether I was serious or just putting on an act, he responded, at first, a little guardedly. But as he spoke, he got so carried away with his own brilliance that all scales of mistrust fell from his voice.

"Well Professor, I first went over to the American Center and checked up about this writer, this, this, Raymond Chandler, in their library. I also tried to read some highfalutin stuff about this Marlowe fellow and what some critic called, let me see, I wrote it down in my notebook. Ah, here it is: 'An analysis of the Philip Marlowe persona excavated via the Los Angeles ambience.' Whew! Who reads such complicated essays? And that author actually got a Ph.D. because of such stuff. It says so, right on the blurb. And that's only *one* essay! Anyway, I couldn't go beyond his first paragraph. But this much

I gathered that the author had settled in LA and that all his books were based on LA itself."

"Elementary, my dear Bhagdig," I egged him on mock-heroically, resurrecting another great detective. "Pray continue, my good man. Now, do I sense some further mischief afoot?"

"You ARE all right, Professor aren't you?" he enquired in an equally mock-solicitous tone." Or should I surprise you still with my yet to be seen Bhagdigian detective powers?"

"Surprise me, O cantankerous sleuth of Sunday mornings," I rhapsodised, getting more and more into the spirit of the game.

"Okay. You asked for it, Professor. Now, sit back and observe! As I was sitting there, my eyes fell on the Calendar section of last week's *LA Times*. One article particularly caught my eye. It was about a...a...let me see my notebook again. About, about, ah, here it is, about all these fictionalised detectives, they do have strange names, ah here it is...the... The Sherlock Holmes Society called the...the..."Calabash Irregulars". Now what in the world is a Calabash?

"Anyway, it seems that every year people from all over the world gather in LA to participate in a week-long festival held in the memory of this great detective, this Holmes fellow. There are book exhibits, seminars, film shows, and even enactments of some of his famous cases. It's almost like a pilgrimage to the shrine of a great hero. Really, all this fuss they make, and that too over bloody characters in a book!"

"Don't worry, Bhagdig. After *you* are gone, our city will also honour you, once every year, exactly in the same way as LA honours Holmes."

"But that's exactly it," Bhagdig piped up excitedly as I mournfully watched my sarcasm literally creep back into its corner like a crestfallen puppy, curl up and fall asleep.

"I got this, this, sudden inspiration of inventing, for Saklatvalla's benefit and for mine, a Philip Marlowe Society, and exactly on the same terms! Don't you see? It would meet once a year, for a whole week, say in a fortnight from today, in LA? Sometimes, I'm surprised by my own brilliance. Look, I'll propose to the old man that as his stolen book was a very rare volume, it is bound to turn up in LA, especially during this special Philip Marlowe festival. And whoever the thief is, he will sell it to the trustees of that Society for a very large sum of money. Now, if Saklatvalla was to send me there in person, mind you, in person, I'd not only alert the trustees of such a venture but I would also be able to catch the thief *and* get the precious volume back. Now I could always pick up another volume of that sort, I'm sure, in a good second-hand bookshop there.

"America is famous for having lots of them and I'm told there are lots of them there who especially sell first-edition volumes. I could easily get the signature of that original publisher forged and then return it to old Saklatvalla in exactly the same condition as he had lost it. I love to scribble on books too, Professor. Especially the ones I'm never likely to read!"

It was the most absurd story I had ever heard. "My dear man, do you think Saklatvalla, of all people, is going to fall for such a cock-and-bull story?" I burst out. "He'll want to know whether such a Society actually exists. He'll ask for all kinds of…of…evidence. Good God, man, he'll ask for several articles, reviews. He will want to see several photographs, you know, all *those* kinds of visible proof that will convince him that such a Society actually exists. Parsis are generous, Bhagdig, but they don't finance trips to L.A. at the drop of a local detective's *topi*!"

But this seemed to increase my friend's enthusiasm all the more. "Exactly! Exactly! Don't you see, that's exactly where *you* come in. I want *you* to write a couple of small interesting pieces on this fictitious Society's existence. You are familiar with the Marlowe fellow. Here. I've made Xerox copies of that LA newspaper article. I'll give them to you. You can use them as a model. I have an old Parsi projectionist friend, Gustadji. Do you know him? He used to work at Edward Theatre. He has a lot of movie stills of old actors and actresses who became famous for resurrecting popular characters on screen. He used to do a little business on the side selling them to Anglo-Indian families in the Railway Colony at Ghorpuri. Used to go to Poona, every weekend, especially for that. Amazingly enterprising, this community of yours, Professor."

"Well, I contacted him, and he was willing to sell me a number of stills of all the famous Hollywood actors who have portrayed this Marlowe fellow in Hollywood films. Now, once we have all the material, I'll get them printed exactly in the same type and lettering of the *L.A. Times Calendar* section."

"Don't tell me! Let me guess: you have another friend," I groaned, "another Parsi who'll do it for you."

"Yes, sir!" he replied proudly. "I do have a friend, but, sadly, he's *not* a Parsi! But, he is an amazing chap. He's the PRO of one of our city's most respected water-cooler companies. He's very good. He won't ask questions. From time to time, we do each other a lot of favours. What do you say, Professor? Will you do it?"

I looked at him and then immediately stretched out my hand. He was delighted. I had to hand it to him. It was a long shot, a very long shot, but it just might work. Besides, nobody was getting hurt in the bargain. Old Saklatvalla did have a lot of money. One constantly saw his photo in the Parsi newspaper *Jam-e-Jamshed*, triumphantly leading his champion race horse "Manecklow" to the padlock. I started. So *that's* why he called his horse by that absurd name! How *low* could one get in raising one's horse above one's father! But I chuckled, nevertheless.

And as for Bhagwat, alias Bhagdig, who sat opposite me still picking his toes, the trip to LA would indeed do *him* a world of good, not only health wise but profession wise also. To solve a case in your own city is one thing. But to solve it in a city thousands of miles away would definitely double his reputation and triple his clientele in Bombay. For me, a little deceit on my part, and I could keep that rare volume of Chandler which indeed I *had* stolen! Hadn't my great detective friend justified my actions, even over the white ants? That way I wouldn't feel any guilt about it at all. And who knows what Saklatvalla would have done with that heirloom if he *had* ever got it back. I'm sure he would have his horse Manecklow trample it to a pulp under his derby sharpened hoofs.

Not only did I agree with my friend but, the coming Wednesday, I also took Bhagdig to the Ripon Club for a sumptuous meal of the city's best-prepared *dhansak* and kebabs. We promised to meet on Friday when I would have the articles typed and ready. The printing would be done over the weekend and the following Tuesday we would spring our little clever enterprise on old Saklatvalla himself.

~

It took me an hour to find Café Aflatoon. I was expected to meet Bhagdig there the following Friday. It was thick in the middle of Bombay's most congested areas—Dhobi Talao. But as I stepped into that small Irani café, I was pleasantly surprised. At the *gullah* stood a tall thin man in a blazing yellow shirt, reading a volume of haiku poetry! Now I have known a lot of Irani weight-lifters, boxers, body-builders, hockey-players, ice-makers, bread-bakers, but never any haiku poetry readers. This was indeed one of those rare epiphanies that only a city like Bombay could produce. So I sat down quietly in the corner and watched him.

The young man's concentration in the noisy din of that cafe was enviable. Every time he read something interesting, he made a loud clicking sound, dialled a number with his long, trembling fingers, and spoke excitedly to someone over the wires. Suddenly, a harsh scream of brakes made me jump out of my seat. A small battered cab came to its heart-failing pant just outside the cafe. With great difficulty, its door was wrenched open and out stepped my fat friend and mentor, perspiring heavily. The driver, a short sallow individual, saluted him wearily and plunged his tottering miracle on wheels expertly into the dense disorder of normal Dhobi Talao traffic.

"Have you another deal going with the cab driver that he gives you free rides?" I blandly enquired as Bhagdig settled his large body on the chair next to mine.

"No, Professor," he said. "I once saved him from having his license revoked. It would have cost him 200 rupees to get it back. So I made a deal with him. If I got back his license, he would give me 200 rupees worth of free rides. That, Professor, was only my 63rd rupee ride."

The man never ceased to amaze me. We ordered hot *mawa* and *chai*. Everyone in the cafe seemed to know him.

An old man whom I had observed doing frantic calculations on a dirty piece of silver cigarette-wrap paper, slid furtively towards Bhagdig and whispered something in his ear. Bhagdig smiled, took the paper from his hand and wrote the number 11 on it. The man snatched his pencil from Bhagdig, crumpled the paper into a ball and thrust it into a small pocket inside his waistband. Then, glancing quickly around, he melted back into the shadows of the cafe's interior.

Bhagdig gave a muffled chuckle and whispered into my astonished ears. "That *bawa* once used to be the head of the Mathematics Department of one of our well-known colleges before the numbers game claimed him. But he's still at it, Professor. Never say die. Figures are in his blood. As I told you, yours is a very enterprising community."

A feverish political argument now broke out somewhere at the back of the room. Seated around the proverbial Irani marble table were four of the most animated old men of Bombay I had ever seen. One of them was so engrossed in castigating his neighbour that he had taken out his dentures and was flourishing them below the other's nose. "That's what our government looked like under the Janata rule. Look at my mouth, look at it, you mollycoddled mothball."

"Why, you, you old fool," replied the other, unwinding the thick scarf that he had wrapped around his head. "You always had a mother complex. *Mataji* this and *Mataji* that. Yes, *Mataji*. No, *Mataji*. What has your *Mataji* done for you ever since she was re-elected the PM? Last year, our railway passes cost 35 rupees. Have you seen today's paper, you toothless old gumboil? From next month, we'll have to pay 85 rupees for them. Your Railway Minister fixed that with your *Mataji*'s government's blessing."

"Interesting bunch of entertainers, aren't they, Professor,"

I knew I could rely on Bhagdig to begin my sentimental Bombay education.

"For the past 25 years that I've been coming here, I've never seen them miss one single evening. No, sir! They are all retired now, but every evening you'll see them here. Two of them come from as far as Borivli and Virar. That toothless fellow comes all the way from Kalyan, but this is their unofficial *adda*. Here, they discuss everything that is currently happening in our Hindustan. They curse, shout, heckle and then quietly take their very last locals home."

"Wonder what will happen to them, Bhagdig, when death starts slowly emptying their ranks?" It was a sad thought on my part to offer him, but suddenly the old men had become very precious to me, almost like Cézanne's card-players.

"There will be no dreamers then left to continue the dream, I guess, Professor," he replied softly.

But then came the business-at-hand voice of Bhagdig and the old men's arguments receded gradually to a murmur. "Dreams aside, let's see the devil's handiwork, shall we, Professor?"

I handed him the articles I had sweated over during the last few days. He read them very carefully. He asked me the meaning of a couple of words, made me simplify a few, and then reread them to himself in a low monotone to see if they sounded right. A couple of more revisions, two cups of *chai*, four additional cakes, and he was finally satisfied. "Now I have to sit on Tryluck's head to get them appropriately designed in the proper layout and print."

"Is that his real name," I innocently enquired, "or is it the name of the famous water-cooler company for which your friend works?"

"You must admit I have original friends, Professor," whispered Bhagdig. "His company's called Pahaadi Paani Limited. Tryluck's real name is Tipu Theekedaar but everyone calls him Tryluck because he's game for anything.

"I went over to meet him yesterday. Thank God he was sober. He had assured all his admirers that he wouldn't touch hooch till the Chinchpokli Darts Contest was over. He's been reigning champion there for the last two years now, and we are all betting heavily on him to regain the title this year as well."

"You require a steady hand and a clear head for that sort of thing, Bhagdig. How on earth will he manage to win if he hits the bottle so regularly? Doesn't his drinking affect his aim?" I whispered back, getting into the spirit of the game.

"He stays in top form, Professor, by aiming at his landlady." Bhagdig watched with amusement as his words struck home. Before I could protest, he threw a few more of his own darts, compelling me to listen with stupefied amazement.

"His landlady, Professor, happens to be one of those grand sirens of our old, old Hindi silent movies." I noticed with pride Bhagdig's use of the word "siren" whose meaning I had just, a few minutes back, explained to him when he came across it in one of my articles. "She and Tryluck are forever fighting. One day it's her dog. Another day it's his motorbike. But in spite of all this, she has a peculiar fondness for him.

"It seems, one day, they had a terrific row over something. As he was about to vacate her premises, she went over to his room and begged him not to. Put on a real performance, so Tryluck told me. 'Don't leave me, Tipu,' she pleaded. 'Don't ever leave, Tryluck. You, you remind me so much, so much of our *purana* Bombay talkies.'

"Poor Tryluck. He's still not figured *that* one out. Come to think of it? Neither have I. Anyway, he got so upset over this outburst that he rushed off to Gustadji and got one of her film-posters. He mounted that on cardboard and made a practice dart-board out of it."

This is something I have to see, I thought to myself, enjoying and loving these eccentric passions of these rare Bombayites I could never have even dreamed of ever meeting had it not been for my friend, beaming at me from across the table. Respectability deprives us of so many interesting facets of life, doesn't it?

"He practises furiously now for two hours every day. And on the day of the tournament, he deliberately picks a fight with her and storms out of her room. Of course, when he comes back, he proudly has the trophy. It's a strategy that just hasn't failed so far. She, of course, doesn't know that. And it's better that way. So if you ever bump into her when we go to meet him, don't ever mention anything about darts. She's a good investment for all of us who lay the bets. Besides..."

"Can I lay a small sum of 25 rupees too, Bhagdig, on Tryluck Thekedaar, to win this year's championship also?"

Bhagdig doubled up with laughter, slapping his knee joyously.

"Let's drink to that, Sam. Now that is what I call an *usli* Parsi *baccha*."

"O, by the way, Bhagdig," I reminded him, "you won't have to go searching for that rare edition of Chandler's in LA. I've made arrangements with an ex-student of mine, Jaffar Mian, to get it for you. He's the manager of the MOSTLY BOOKS bookshop. It's near the Stock Exchange in Chicago Radio Lane. We'll go there one day to collect your precious parcel. It's a very interesting bookshop, probably Bombay's finest.

"And Jaffar Mian, God bless the boy, you'll like him. He's worked his way very hard to get a Bachelor's Degree in Literature in my college. Although he got a third class, he was one of my best students, Bhagdig. His English, even today, may not be all that good, but he really loves the subject. Not like the other pampered brats who took it just to show it off in polite society. To have become a manager of one of our finest bookshops is really no mean achievement, especially when you have stayed in a crowded noisy chawl; when you have had to walk to college on certain days for miles and miles because you didn't have the bus fare; when you have had to study under the dim lights of the nearest petrol-pump station because the family couldn't afford the expensive electricity bill; when you have always managed to pay your college tuition fees on time by teaching some of our city's notorious smugglers how to read the daily English newspaper for two hours every morning, five days of the week!"

Bhagdig's eyes softened. For a moment I saw a sudden hint of tears.

I was surprised at my own self for having got carried away over Jaffar Mian. The reason was quite simple. For an ex-professor, that too of an obsolete subject like Literature in India, there are practically no rewards except that elusive, that rare, almost non-existent student who shows a genuine love and devotion for the subject. Jaffar Mian had been my only rewarding pupil in my long and undistinguished career. But the fact that I could share so rare a secret with someone else came as a complete surprise, even to me.

"Professor," Bhagdig's voice shook a little as he clasped both my hands in his. "I may have more friends than you, but what you just said of Jaffarmian stands much higher, yes, head and shoulders above all my friends, above all what we call ordinary friendships. It is not a common thing to be proud of one's real friends, Professor, because sometimes we spend our entire life looking for them and not finding them."

"I have more than one real friend now," I said quietly.

"And may he never betray that trust, Professor," he answered.

We were both silent. Any more words would have spoilt it but never was the silence so wonderful between two old men: one who had seen so much of the world and one who had seen practically nothing. One of us had to break the spell if that moment had to be possessed and retained. This time, for a change, I decided to take the initiative.

"Jaffar Mian told me that a big shipment of smuggled books is expected soon. He has already placed our order for that rare Chandler volume. You'll have to wait a little, but I'm sure by the time you return from L.A., he'll have the book for you. Now I must go. I'm getting late. I have to see a French film at the Alliance Françaises. Would you like to walk with me to Marine Lines?"

"No, Professor. I'll sit here. I'm quite tired. Besides, in a few minutes my trusted cab will arrive. I have some plans for the evening also. They are more of...the flesh-and-blood type." He grinned wickedly, gathering up the cake crumbs from the table in his palm and then scooping them into his mouth.

"Blood is always thicker than water, eh Bhagdig. Now restrain yourself in your 64th rupee cab ride. Don't do anything that Maneckshaw wouldn't have done with the ladies."

Bhagdig snorted and gave a whooping cough of a laugh. The old men who had been arguing fiercely turned around and glared at us. The young haiku reader smiled shyly at us and went on reading. Bhagdig got up and escorted me out. A thin drizzle had just started. I hailed a cab and got in.

"Till next Tuesday then, Professor. Meet me at the entrance of the Saklatvalla Library. And enjoy your French film. Not censored, is it? Ah, ha! Let me know if it had a lot of 'those' scenes in it."

I laughed. He patted me on the arm and slowly went back towards the café.

~

The lift wheezed just a little as it took us to Mr. Saklatvalla's office. The man who operated the machine was an old Parsi. He was wearing dirty white pants, and an equally filthy shirt with an over-tight black coat covering it. His frayed black prayer *topi* was perched cock-eyed on his head. His pants, I noticed and so did Bhagdig as he nudged me, were kept in place by the sacred thread of his faith—the *kasti*—here used as a belt to prevent any indecent exposure. He couldn't speak much because he had pockets of snuff tucked away in that weird hollow terrain of his mouth. When he did smile, which was quite often, I saw bent and crooked teeth, very few of them, jutting out of his snuff-smeared gums like crazily tilting tombstones. Yet, what pains he took to keep his little cage, clean, tidy and polished.

The old-fashioned lever was Brasso-ed to a perfect shine and he handled it proudly, like a rich millionaire would his yacht. The company's name—Lockley & Hudson—shone brightly on its plaque. As we leisurely went up, I could see the well-greased wheels over which the strong pulley cords were yanking us up. Through the grilled enclosure I passed the grand stone staircase, a trifle dirty, with its innumerable marble busts on each floor of all those venerable Parsi scions of the Saklatvalla family. It was nice to travel in a cage which for once didn't have all those threatening buttons and multi-coloured knobs that shot you up and dropped you down with a terrifying clockworked efficiency.

The old man sat on a pillow carefully placed on his stool. If only he was dressed a little neater, but somehow he managed to convey the impression that it was *his* 'lift' you were expected to admire and not him! He glided it to a hushed halt, as skillfully and coaxingly as an Anglo-Indian engine-driver bringing his roaring steam-engine to a stop, just at the edge of the railway station platform. He didn't yank open the door for us to get out. He merely gave it a push. Like a faithful guardian who had deposited his wards, down he went for the upteenth time to fetch yet another hurried, harassed soul from the stressed depths of the city.

We had hardly taken two steps towards the main office when there was a considerable roar, and an old Parsi couple suddenly staggered out. The man was weeping copiously and the woman was trying her best to console him. It was a sight that could have stopped anyone in their tracks. The woman finally pulled the man to an empty bench, sat down beside him and tried to wipe away his tears. He had the most amazingly combed curly hair that I had ever seen, all Brilliantine-d back from his forehead. He had a faded old green shirt on which he had pinned a broad yellow tie full of horseshoes. An ancient string of heavy gold buttons stood at attention all the way down his shirtfront. The enormous pocket of his shirt bulged with a battalion of six different pens, behind which was cushioned a slightly dog-eared kerchief, neatly folded. His frayed colourless tweed coat was comically patched at the elbow, back and neck with pink quilt cloth and his striped pants, a little too short, had been given, one could see, a skillfully disguised sewn-up job. Sheer dandyism was resorted to in order to cover up the tragic wear and tear of a dignity not willing to be surrendered yet, to poverty, and he moved both of us very much. We instinctively went towards the couple.

The woman blew his nose, straightened up and put a strong, reassuring hand on the old man's sobbing shoulders. She was tiny, but one could see, much stronger of the two. Her face showed the daily strains of survival. She was dressed in a colourful frock exploding with blue and yellow glittering birds. She had these two schoolgirl plaits of hair, the ends of which were tied tightly with, of all things, shoelaces. She had wonderful eyes—fiery, brown and sparkling. They spoke along with her words that soon sprinkled all over us as we approached them. "That rogue. That beast. What does he think he is? Just because he's Head-Librarian, he has no right, he has no right, to *dhumko* my poor Savaksa. He's worked here for 15 years. He's eaten the old man's *namak*. You gentlemen, you both seem kind people. You're *zhartosti* aren't you, *Mota seth*? And you, Hindu *seth,* are his *dost*? That *dukkar*, that Percy Bamboat is *zhartosti* too! Night and day he bullies him, insults him, calls him all sorts of names. *Toba! Toba!*

"My husband has arthritis, gentlemen. His fingers shake. It takes him a very long time to write all those 'fine' receipts. But he works overtime. He doesn't ask for an extra *paisa*. But today, after all these years, my Savaksa answered him back, and why shouldn't he? Wouldn't you if you were constantly *satao-ed* by that, that...cartoon!

He says he's going to throw Savaksa out. How dare he? Just like that? After 15 years? He's old enough to be his father. He won't get away, I'll speak to Saklatvalla *seth* himself. I'll go to the Parsi Panchayat. I'll telephone—"

"Now look her, Mehramai." It wasn't hard to guess the speaker—*the* Mister Percy Bamboat. He was short, middle-aged and had all the qualities of a transplanted Nazi SS Man. His close-cropped hair stood up on quivering quills of anger. He had the fat neck of a Bhimpura *guli mowali* and his small beady eyes bounced at you like furiously smashed ping-pong balls. His ears that the Maker had hurriedly glued to his sides were red arrow tips of rage and his big rounded face threatened to burst any minute with a fist or a kick coming at you right through its center. He was dressed in over-starched white pants and a bush-shirt. There was not a single white hair on his head. He had four glittering rings wedged tightly in the sausage-like fingers of his right hand which he was waving, dangerously close, just a little above Savaksa's waves and waves of shiny curls.

"What do you think we're running here?" he demanded in the rich resonant voice of a tough PT teacher. "A bloody charity institution? Why don't you tell your lazy layabout sons to work and look after you both in your old age?

"And what does your husband think he is, John Barrymore? He spends more time in the bathroom arranging the curls on his head than working behind his fines counter. Every time a pretty girl stands in line to pay the library fine, he rushes to the bathroom. At his age—"

"Look here Bamboat," I bristled, "that's no way to speak to these people."

"It's *Mister* Percy Bamboat to you, old man. And mind your own business. Just what gives you the right to talk to me like that?" he snapped back.

"Careful *bawaji*, careful," interrupted Bhagdig. "We shouldn't talk to our old teachers like that. This is my friend, Professor Bijlikhan. I hope you remember *me* at least. You don't? I'm private detective Bhagdig. Remember, I met you a couple of days ago in Mr. Saklatvalla's office? I'm investigating the theft of that rare volume which I believe you *failed* to report to Mr. Saklatvalla till one of your *own* members brought it to your notice? That's not nice, *bawaji*, that's not nice."

"Yes. I remember you. And I don't need *you* to tell *me* how to do my job. And stop calling me *bawaji*. Private detective indeed! Go and chase some divorce cases." Bamboat's snappy judgment of people was certainly vivid but that did not deter Bhagdig at all.

"What *do* you do, Head-Librarian," he taunted Percy. "Trample old people's toes or play the numbers, maybe in your spare time?"

"Hear, hear," I said. "Come, Mehramai, and you too, Savaksa. Don't worry. Although my friend is not a *zhartosti*, he and I will see how this *mowali* drives you out. We're here to meet Mr. Saklatvalla. And he's a good *zhartosti* isn't he? Then why do you worry? We'll plead on your behalf. Go to the nearby *agyari* and sit before the *atas* and just imagine all of us roasting our fat friend here over the sandalwood. God also has a sense of humour, you know. Meet us here in an hour, okay? Now, now, don't worry. Today is *hormuzd rooj*. Nothing inauspicious can happen to the good on this day. Don't you know that? Of course, you do. Come on, now. Cheer up. Cheer up."

"God bless you, sir," said old Savaksa. "God bless you too, Detective *sahib*. We'll go and pray. May Ahura Mazda protect us from such *Aoorimaans*. Come Mehra, come darling. And thank you again, Sirs, thank you again. Come sweetheart, the lift has arrived."

"What are you gaping at, Bamboat?" Bhagdig's voice thundered ominously so that everyone around could hear it. "Go and see whether some more rare books have been stolen or not during the time you were bullying these old people."

Bamboat did a rapid nose dive into his rage again. Then standing on the top of his toes, he hissed at us. "I'll see that both of you are thrown out from here. Immediately. Now. I'll, I'll speak to Mr. Saklatvalla right this minute, you hear, right this minute."

"Go right ahead, Percy boy," I encouraged him. "Go right ahead. But we'll be right behind your heels. Right behind."

"Remember that, *bawaji*," added Bhagdig (how well we worked as a team), "remember that. We haven't finished playing snakes and ladders with you, yet!"

~

All three of us burst into Saklatvalla's room just when the old man was holding a small tin-cup into which his parrot was emptying its last digestive litter. "Don't you knock anymore, gentlemen?" he hesitatingly enquired. "What is it this time, Percy? Why, Mr. Bhagdig, you're, you're early. Come on, Malcolm birdee, hurry up, will you. I haven't got all day. Please, please, sit down gentlemen, and Percy, will you, will you stop walking up and down. Really. You wear out my carpet and my patience. Are you done, Malcolm? Good. If you'll just excuse me, gentlemen, I'll empty this..."

"Why don't you give that cup to our dear Head-Librarian here, Mr. Saklatvalla. I'm sure dear Percy won't mind. Would you Percy?" It had been a long time since I had made a boy stand up on a bench in class as punishment.

Percy's face quickly burst into sullen rainbow colours. He was about to explode but instead, found a small tin cup pressed into his hand. "Here, Percy, just, just empty it outside, will you. There's…there's no need to…er... wash it. Just bring it back as it is. I didn't catch your name, Mr.—Mr.…."

"Bijlikhan, Mr. Saklatvalla." Bhagdig interposed for me. "Professor Sam Bijlikhan, retired. Used to teach English at Loyola College. He's helping me with the case of our stolen book. He feels its loss painfully too."

"That's very, er...very handsome of...of you, Professor," Saklatvalla got up and shook my hand. Just then Percy entered, looking quite absurd with that tiny emptied tin-cup in his fat trembling fingers.

"Conspiring behind my back, are you?" he thundered. "These, these two men, Mr. Saklatvalla, they had the nerve to insult me right now before the whole staff, especially before Savaksa and Mehramai. Mr. Saklatvalla, I'm afraid I'll *have* to fire Savaksa. He's getting—he's getting too old and too obstinate for his boots. Why, just the other day he, he..."

"Percy," an exasperated Mr. Saklatvalla interrupted him, "I have some private business with with—these two gentlemen. Would you mind coming back in, say, in 15 minutes. Then we'll talk about Savaksa. Here, while we're talking, go to Suklaajee Street and buy me some...some bird grain for Malcolm, will you!"

It just wasn't poor Percy's day. Muttering venomous curses on parrots, professors, and detectives, he stormed out to buy bird-grain for his employer who sank back with temporary relief in his enormous rocking chair.

Bhagdig, quick to seize this opportunity immediately launched into his LA narrative. I have to admit, it was an excellent performance. Even a transplanted Socrates would have been proud of Bhagdig's shrewd native rhetoric. I, of course, discreetly kept to my prompter's box, waiting for Bhagdig's calculatedly strewn pregnant pauses. And when they came, I quickly filled them in with all the factual evidence of that notoriously fictitious Philip Marlowe Society we had resurrected somewhere in Pasadena, LA. After our virtuoso performance was over, we sank back into our chairs and waited for Old Saklatvalla's verdict.

It came, but rather as a sentence. "My dear fellows, after all the trouble you, you both have taken, I, I hate to disappoint you. I just received a...a letter from the original publishers of that...that damned volume. I had written to them enquiring about the existence of, of another... er...rare first edition. One of them, remembered my, my late father. It seems my late father had...er...managed to save him from a...a delicate situation. So, in return, he has...er, promised to send me his...his own copy. It's...it's already on its way. But I didn't know this Marlowe fellow was so, so well-liked. Really, to have a...a whole Society and, and, have all these...functions?"

Poor Bhagdig. I could see his face slowly crumble and come to rest on one of his many chins. Even I felt very crestfallen. And to darken our horizon even further, who would choose to open the door and make an entrance, just at that moment, but Percy, holding disdainfully in his two hands, two large bags of bird-grain. As he placed them, rather, banged them down on Saklatvalla's desk, Bhagdig, who had been slouching in his chair, suddenly seemed to straighten up. There was a touch of resolute colour on his face once again. And it was as though in a dream I heard Bhagdig say, "But there is still the matter of the person who *stole* your heirloom in the first place, Mr. Saklatvalla. I know who the thief is. He is right here, right here in this very room."

Surely he was not going to turn *me* in? Not after all the work I had done for him? Human nature is such a funny thing. This man, whom I had admired these past few days, suddenly became ugly, threatening. Maybe he had a deal going with Saklatvalla on the side I knew nothing of. I felt cheated, hurt. I was about to rise and defend myself when Bhagdig, true to his flair for dramatics, took the small tin-cup from Saklatvalla's desk and flung it at Percy Bamboat.

"That's your man, Mr. Saklatvalla. That's your rotten *chor*!"

"What nonsense are you talking?" Percy Bamboat's face, purple to its roots, crackled like a frying pan on which Bhagdig seemed to have broken an unexpected egg. Then, turning to Mr. Saklatvalla, he controlled his anger and in a ruffled boy-scout tone said, "Mr. Saklatvalla, I've served you faithfully for the last 17 years, and you allow this, this *jassoos* fellow to insult me like this? Really, sir, I'll tender my resignation than stand accused of robbery!"

"You won't have to Bamboat," continued Bhagdig calmly. "I'll see that you're fired instead of honest men like Savaksa and if you don't go quietly then..."

"Just a minute, just a minute, Mr. Bhagdig. What, er, proof do you have that...that—er... Percy here is, is involved in, in all this...er...mess?" asked the utterly confused Mr. Saklatvalla, whose mind must have been going around in circles, as indeed was mine.

"Last Friday, Mr. Saklatvalla," pronounced Bhagdig, producing his aces slowly and deliberately in the familiar manner of most paperback hack sleuths, "I went out and talked to one, Fatima Lobo. You don't know her, gentlemen, but our Percybaba does. In fact they once were very close, were you not, lover boy?

"Our Percybaba, gentlemen, is quite a character. Do you know that he sells bogus homeopathy pills outside one of our city's respected *agyaris*? He even has a flourishing business going on inside that place of worship. Percybaba has a finger there, gentlemen, in everything: from selling sandalwood to charging 30 per cent commission for every prayer offered by some of those *dasturjis* there in honour of the departed."

"Your Parsi Panchayat should look into this racket, Mr. Saklatvalla. Aren't you one of the presiding members there?"

The speed at which Bhagdig hurled Fatimas, sandalwood and homeopathy pills at poor Saklatvalla, made him more and more confused about this 'mess' as he called it. "Yes, yes," he replied to Bhagdig, "but who is this, this Lobo woman, and how did you come by, all this, this, er information about one of our, our..."

"A woman scorned doesn't keep her trap, excuse me, her mouth shut, Mr. Saklatvalla. Our lover boy changes women as frequently as he changes his bush shirts. It seems, gentlemen, lover boy here had promised to take Fatima to the Carnival at Goa, but at the last moment ditched her for someone else. When I asked her what they had quarrelled about, she confessed, that lover boy here had stolen some rare book from the library. He had wanted her to take this book to a particular smuggler's hut at Dharavi, and when Fatima had refused and called him a 'coward' for not doing so himself, and you should have heard all the other titles she gave him, he threw her out. Yes, gentlemen, he threw her out just like a *dhobi*'s *gatri*. On top of that, Fatima told me, he even refused to pay her the money he had borrowed from her and..."

"That's a bloody lie," shouted Percy. "Fatima and I had a quarrel but it was..."

"Ah, so you do admit knowing this Lobo woman, don't you?" Saklatvalla piped in.

"So what," Percy shot back in his usual Bamboat rubber-band fashion, "*your* father knew a lot of women living in that lane too!"

Mr. Saklatvalla stood up trembling like a foot ruler itching to come down on a subordinate's palm: "Mr. Percy Bamboat, how dare you? How dare you disturb the...the... ashes of a dead man? You are *fired*, you hear. I want you *out* of here, this, this very minute. And if you ever, ever set foot in my...my library again or, or even come near my, my late father's marble bu...bu...bust, I'll, I'll serve a notice, yes, a legal notice on you. No wonder, you, you, didn't report the theft imme...immediately to, to me."

"Hear, hear," I applauded Mr. Saklatvalla's righteous indignation. "And Percy boy, you won't have ever to empty a parrot's litter again or be caught at Suklajee Street with bird-grain in your hands."

All three of us burst into laughter. Percy bellowed and stamped out like a bull with three picador lances sticking out from his fat thug's neck. So ferocious was his exit that before he left the room he vented all his unspoken anger on an old innocent-looking hat-rack on which his employer's coat and hat were hanging. He flung it down so violently that it landed with a heavy crash right on top of Saklatvalla's glass fish aquarium. We all jumped from our seats and rushed to the poor air-choked fish that lay on the carpet gasping and writhing for water.

"Dear, dear," moaned poor Mr. Saklatvalla, surveying the damage in his room. "I'll have to get a new glass case for my fish soon, and...and advertise for a new Head Librarian all, all over again. I'll have to ask my wife and, and other trustees to...to...sit in for the…the interview. No, no wonder those damned ho...ho...homeop...pathy pills didn't work. Charged me double for…for them. The scoundrel! Now what else do…do you want, you silly bird? You, you want to relieve yourself a...a...gain?!"

Holding our laughter as tightly as we could, we sneaked out of Mr. Saklatvalla's chamber. The whole office staff had gathered outside, including a beaming Mehramai and Savaksa. We were welcomed as heroes who had succeeded in getting rid of that Bamboatian sphinx who had dragonised them for so many years.

They were all old, poor, shabbily dressed Parsis, but the love and affection that flowed from their ravaged faces and bent frames would have awakened any cynical god who had shut his eyes in despair at what his world had done to them. They wouldn't let us go before they had sweetened our mouths with delicious Parsi delicacies bought for us especially from the excellent Ratan Tata Institute. It must have cost each of them an expensive rupee, but it showed they cared.

Even the old liftman who took us down suddenly became a charioteer, escorting his heroes back into the lively Bombay street from a well-deserved victory at the battlefield. "I *refoosed* to take Mr. Bumboat down in my lift. *Sala haramkhor*! *Zhartosti*s like him should be sent back to Iran or whipped in the marketplace like they used to in the British Raj. God bless you, gentlemen. God bless you!"

~

Bhagdig was strangely silent as we slowly walked down Flora Fountain. A lot of American tourists were crowded curiously before the large display windows of the Khadi Emporium. Two ostentatiously meek salespeople, a man and a woman, were in the process of adjusting the loin-cloth and the *dhoti* of a terribly un-Gandhian mannequin. I had *always* strongly disapproved of making one of our great leaders a saleable commodity, especially before tourists who were still trying to historically figure him out! Once, I had even picked a fight with one of those so-called sermon-mouthing ashramites when he had tried to sell me a pair of *Kohlapuri chappal*s by insisting that it was *the* pair Vallabhbhai Patel had used on one of his British jailers! True to the Bijlikhan credo, I had vindicated poor Patel's apocryphal behaviour by using the same pair on that unfortunate salesman himself.

I wonder which bird-brain thought of such gimmicks. I was about to make a remark when I noticed that friend Bhagdig had not stopped at all and was standing a little apart, with downcast eyes, waiting for me to catch up.

I decided to go and cheer him up. So what if LA had been snatched away from him. Hadn't he got his man? "There's nothing to be so disappointed about, *dost*," I began gaily. "LA was not worth all that effort anyway. Percy Bamboat was, wasn't he? Didn't you see the look of love, of admiration, of triumph on the faces of all those old Parsis, especially, especially old Savaksa and Mehramai? That is your reward, Bhagdig. The lesser Bamboats there are in this world, the better. So what if you framed him. He's not going to starve. He's got his homeopathy pills, and his fire-temple racket. It's poetic justice that prompted you to lie. It saved not only poor Saavaksa, but *me* too. After all I did steal the vo..."

"It's not that at all, Professor," Bhagdig replied slowly. "It was the look on *your* face when I told Old Saklatvalla I knew who the thief was that has upset me so much. How could you, Sam? How could you, even for a moment, think I was going to expose you! That is what hurt me. I do make deals to get what I want. It's a tough city we both live in, Professor. A man has to make deals if he lives by his wits. But those deals are not to hurt my own friends. You are my friend. How could you even dream that I would turn *you* in? And before Saklatvalla, of all people? Just because he was paying me? And before Bamboat, that rogue?"

I had never seen Bhagdig get so emotional, and he was right. How blind I had been. I rushed to embrace him. "I'm sorry Bhagdig. I'm really, really sorry. It was unpardonable on my part. I guess human nature got the better of me as it sometimes does with all of us. It's just that, well on various occasions I, I...have...been... betrayed—by…by well, but that's all in the past...but still there's this, this tiny space in me, I guess in all of us, that instinctively anticipates yet another betrayal. And don't, don't ever use the past tense when referring to me as your friend, ever again, Bhagdig. I'll, I'll..."

Bhagdig's eyes sparkled again and he returned the embrace.

"But, but, how on earth," I asked Bhagdig getting my breath back, "did you locate this Fatima woman and..."

"In my line of work, Professor," replied Bhagdig, reverting back to the professional tones of the much experienced, much weather-beaten sleuth, "one has to have an alternative plan of action to fall back on, if the first one fails. You know, the first time I was at the library, I had had a very rude reception from our Mister Bamboat. It suddenly struck me that even if he was *not* the thief, he did have excellent qualifications for being one. So I snooped around, talked with the other old people and got a lot of valuable information about him."

"Now, Fatima Lobo used to often come to the library when their *lafda* was going on. She was a very warm and nice woman who soon became quite friendly with the library's staff. Now, when I was told that she had not visited the library for a long time, I assumed that she and Percy must have split. So I bribed one of the old fellows to go and have a word with Fatima and, sort of, prepare the scene for my visit. He came back with the very good news that Fatima was hopping mad at Bamboat and was itching for an opportunity to get back at him for the way he had rejected her. So I went to see her last Friday and we, er, worked out a deal, in case she had to come and swear in court."

"And after that she must have been very generous too, eh, friend Bhagdig?" I inquired.

He chuckled. I couldn't fancy Bhagdig as a lady's man, but maybe in some immediate future, even *that* side of his personality would be revealed to me.

As for Fatima, she interested me too. My unfortunate pride, after a particular day, many years ago had kept me away from women, but Fatima seemed to promise some distinct ancient stirrings. "Why don't you bring Fatima over on Sunday afternoon?" I suddenly asked Bhagdig. "I'll take you both to Ripon Club for lunch. They have a good chicken *vindaloo* that day. Consider that as my reward for bringing your case to a successful conclusion."

~

Sunday morning at 8.30, the phone rang. I stumbled toward the instrument, muttering and cursing.

"Professor? Sam?" said the excited voice of Bhagdig. "Did you read today's *Free Press Journal*? Front page, right hand corner. All four volumes of the...the, one minute, ah here it is. All four volumes of the Hokosaido Publication of the, the *Rare Collected Haiku Poems of the Masters* have been stolen from the Asiatic Library. Could we meet at 9.30 at Café Aflatoon? Fatima has promised to come straight to Ripon at 12.00. This time, I'm sure I'll get to Japan. What do you say? Professor? Sam? Bijlikhan? Hello...are you listening? What? What? O, *you* want to come too! Really? Why, that would be wonderful, wonderful! Let's see, how we'll work this deal out. It'll require careful planning. Hello...hello... Not over the phone? All right, all right, Professor, at 9.30 then."

Laughingly, I put down the receiver and went to the bathroom. I looked at myself in the mirror. I had to prepare a new face to meet the world from now on. I had got fed up of the old one anyway. First Fatima, then a little Lobo-ing, why not, and then, of all places, Japan, Bhagdig, me and Mount Fujiyama. I started shaving. But who on earth in Bombay could have wanted these four volumes of Haiku poetry so desperately? A blazing yellow shirt, trembling fingers dialling the phone...of course! But surely...Bhagdig would work it out all right. He always did.

I smiled and went on shaving._

GLOSSARY

A

aayee	mother in Marathi
achha	all right
adalat	court of law
adda	favourite meeting place
adoo-lasan	ginger and clove
agarbatti	joss stick
agyari	Parsi fire temple
Ahura Mazda	God of Light in Zoroastrianism
ajnabi	strange
amma	mother
ammi jaan	beloved mother in Urdu
angrezi	English
Aoorimaan	Devil in Zoroastrianism
arrey	c'mon
ashem vohu	a Parsi prayer
asli	true
atas	sacred flame
atash	flame
aurat pesha	semblance of womanhood
azad	independent

B

bawaji	mocking honorific for Parsis
baba	son
babu	sir
bacchu	kid
badmash	rascal
badshah	emperor
bali	journey
bangla-gaadi	bungalow and car
bansuri	flute
bapu	father; nickname for Mahatma Gandhi
baugh	autonomous residential complex, built only for poor, middle-class and rich Parsis; many still exist in Bombay, Poona, and other Indian cities
bayloo	emasculated one
begum	wife in Urdu
beta	son
bhag	run
bhagwan	god
bhakrah	sweet Parsi tea-time snack
bhangi	untouchable
bhasha	language
bhau	brother in Marathi
bhel	tasty snack
bijli	lighting
billi	cat
brun	hard Iranian bread
buddhi	inner mind

bungle	room where the last Parsi rites for the dead are performed
bun maska	buttered bun

C

chacha	uncle
chai	tea
chal	come
chamcha	spoon
chamda	leather
chapati	Indian bread
charkha	wheel
chawl	common residence for poor people made up of tiny rooms existing side by side along a long balcony in the front and one at the back where common bathrooms and toilets, assigned to individual families, are located
chee chee gora	Anglo-Indian
chhokra	boy
choola	stove
chor	robber

D

daal chawal	rice and lentils
daru	liquor
desi	local
dhakma	Parsi funeral site
dhandar patya	yellow lentils with spicy sauce—a Parsi dish

dhansak	Sunday traditional Parsi meal of brown rice, *daal*, and kebabs
dhobi	washerman
dhobi's gatri	washerman's load
dhoti	lower garment worn by Hindus
dhumko	to scold
dikra/dikroo	Parsi lad
diwana	mad
doodhified	milky
doodhwali	milkmaid
dost	friend
dosti	friendship
dukkar	pig
dumroo	small drum
dungarwadi	mourning site for Parsis

E

ek mahina	one month
ek numbari	number one

F

farishta	angel
firangi	foreigner
fonny	funny

G

gadha	donkey
gaajar halwa	carrot desert
gaali	slur
gajra	wrist garland

gangajal	sacred water of the Ganges
gatha	Parsi hymn
gavashnee	good thoughts
ghazal	Indian classical music form of singing and poetry
ghoda	horse
gilli-danda	Indian amateur sport played with two wooden sticks
gora	white
grahak	customer
gullah	restaurant till

H

haramkhor	rascal
hamaal	coolie
hatbatti	country hooch
Hindustan	India
hoormuzed rooj	first auspicious day of the Parsi calendar

I

icegosht	frozen mutton
isus	incense
iskerlator	escalator
itvaar	Sunday
izzat	honour

J

jadoo	magic
jassoos	detective
jhagda	fight

K

kaata	fork
kabaddi	Indian wrestling sport played amongst two teams
kajal	kohl
kapda guru	fashion designer
karma	destiny
kasti	sacred thread of the Parsis
kavi	poet
khadi	handspun cloth that Mahatma Gandhi insisted all Indians should wear
khadi bhandar	city emporium
khandyaa	pallbearer
khansama	cook
kismat	luck
kohli	room
kolhapuri chappals	hand-crafted leather slippers, originally from Kolhapur, Maharashtra
kulfi	Indian ice cream
kunashnee	good thought

L

lafda	affair

M

ma-bhen	slurs about mother-sister
machhardani	mosquito net
mai	mother

maidan	playing field
manas	outer mind
manashnee	good deeds
mandir	temple
manjha	cutting thread made in a way that enables a paper kite to duel with another during the kite flying season
masahari	non-vegetarian
masjid	mosque
maska	butter
mataji	respected mother
matric pass	school-leaving certificate
mawa	cake
mian	friend in Urdu
mithaas	sweetness
mithai	sweets
mobed	Parsi priest
mohalla	locality
moksha	liberation
moochi	cobbler
moolga	son
mooniceepul	municipal
mootri	piss
mota seth	respected sir
mowali	thug
muaa	bastard
munshi	marriage broker
muttonwala	butcher

N

naachnewali	dancer
naashatani	drunkard
nakoo	no
namak	salt
narangi	orange hooch
naseeb	luck
Navroze	a Parsi festival
naukri	job
nutkhut tamasha	useless spectacle

O

old and *naya paisa*	Indian currency of the past

P

paan	betel leaf
paanwala	betel nut vendor
pahaadi pani	mountain water
paidus	Parsi funeral procession
paisa	one-hundredth of a rupee
Papeti	a Parsi festival
parivar	family
parmatma	Supreme Being
parmeshwar	God Almighty
Parsi lok	Parsi people
pelate	plate
phoreen	foreign
piglofy	to melt
popatji	sweet Parsi tea-time snack
prasad	religious offering
puppa	father in Parsi
purana	old

Q

qaum	community
qurbani	sacrifice

R

raddi purana	rag and bone
raddiwala	peddler of used goods
rani	queen
rangoli	powdered chalk patterns on the floor
refoosed	refused

S

saal mubarak	Happy New Year in Parsi
sadrakasti	corpse
sahib	sir
sagaa	real
sala	damn
salli	thinly sliced potato fries
sangeet	music
satao-ed	harassed
satyagraha	protest
sawal	question
seth	master
shakahari	vegetarian
sharabi	sod
shastra	sacred Hindu law
shoba	pride
suar	swine
swadeshi	one's own country

T

tamasha	spectacle
tambaku	tobacco
tandava	Shiva's dance of destruction
tareli mucchi	fried fish—a popular Parsi dish
tawaif	whore
taxiwala	cab driver
thali	platter
thayli	bag
toba	shame
tonga	horse-drawn carriage
topi	hat
tukda	piece

U

usli baccha	real kid
ustad	honorific title for a teacher, an artist

V

vilayat	England

Y

yaar	buddy

Z

zhartosti	a Zoroastrian